Remembering
SUMMER JAM 73

Ron Cosentino

Remembering Summer Jam 73
Printed by Yawn Publishing LLC
2555 Marietta Hwy, Ste 103
Canton, GA 30114
www.yawnsbooks.com

Yawn Publishing LLC has formatted and printed this book for the author, who assumes all liability and holds Yawn Publishing LLC harmless and indemnifies them against any claims related to this work and the contents of this book, including, but not limited to, the names used, the accuracy of events, people, and places depicted; opinions expressed; previously published pictures and any other materials.

Library of Congress Control Number: 2023911742

ISBN: 978-1-954617-69-8

Printed in the United States

INTRODUCTION

1973 marked the culmination and the end of the early music scene of the hippie era formulated in California in the mid 1960's. San Francisco had "The Grateful Dead's" house scene at 710 Asbury street, in the Haight Asbury district, a family unit with pranksters. Macon, Georgia had "The Big House,"2321 Vineville street, the residence of The Allman Brothers Band; now a museum dedicated to the music and history of the Allman Brothers Band, their scene in the sleepy city of Macon, Georgia. "The Band" had a house known as "Big Pink" 56 Parnassus Lane, Saugerties, New York; a place to gather; make music, a family atmosphere where Bob Dylan could be at home. All across America there were local scenes where young people congregated to form their own families or congregations of like-minded people. Enjoying life by their own rules, when the grip of law enforcement was limited. American society was learning to grow up, accept the future does not stand still. Life accelerates; morph's into its own inertia, what becomes of it. We cherish the memories and the bonds that were created though our reach with each other has been separated by time, distance, eventually souls move on no longer with us. Our memories linger on. In Edinboro Pennsylvania there was such a house and group metastasized together in the summer of 1973. We knew it as "Char Lynn," a small grey two-story house in Edinboro, Pennsylvania in the northwest corner of Pennsylvania where Edinboro University resides. Then there was "Summer Jam 73" at Watkins Glen racetrack in upstate New York. The story now being told, how 30 people traveled from Edinboro, Pennsylvania to the mega concert in 24-foot rental truck. What happened on the way to Watkins Glen is beyond belief, it happened; story be told, is here for you to read and enjoy. There will never be another year like 1973, a time of peace, joy and freedom.

CHAPTER ONE

Destination Unknown

The quintessential Rock and Roll story for the ages

Leaving home for the first time after high school graduation; I don't know where I'm going, I don't know what I need. Expectations or the best of plans turn into flying by the seat of one's pants; for others it would be "Winging it," same thing. Disciplined people advance like it is another form of education, using the same formula that worked in high school. I would press the envelope, come what may. Adjustments on the fly, no landing gear for when things go wrong; inevitably do. Nothings for certain; it can all go wrong, or the magic of life appears. Threshold of what will be.

It's not the fall that makes you, it's the bounce takes you to your next decision, destination. I don't know where I'm gonna end up. I will keep moving on. Live for each experience without hesitation. Life is about the decisions we make, our choices. If one never ventures out, taking a chance on themselves, their dreams, believing you can. The escape will be the ghost you never know. Never pursue a life that would make me ordinary. Can't never did nothing.

Without contemplation, no reliable plan, I would let life come to me. The evolution of it all. A free spirit, free to be me. Too many things I wanted to experience going about life in a conventional manor. It has its prominence, a place, in a loving society. That was for the worker ants, I wanted to be a King Bee. Wanting to be so many things, experience as many events and accomplishments as they presented themselves to my sense of challenge and resolve.

I picked my opportunities as they came along; some I managed to will into reality, others swept me away. I tried

1

everything in my life; the things I liked, I tried twice. Free on my own, the way it was meant to be, free to be me. This is a story that should be told. Welcome to my world, won't you come on in.

The first thing gone wrong, being admitted to college with no dormitory room available for me, a place I could call home. Admitted late into the system. Consequently, I found myself living the military life in the basement of Schaefer Hall on the campus of Edinboro State College. Now known as Edinboro University, in the northwest corner of the state of Pennsylvania. In that large room, more than 100 male students slept on mattresses on the floor: barracks style. Youth on our side, got all the time in the world.

The school's housing department forced students double up, per dormitory room; effectively making them live like sardines in a can. Getting to know you. It happened that way in some of the girls dorms as well. Even the infirmary was loaded down with female students not having a place to board up. They did keep two of the twenty-four beds in the infirmary available for people who really needed medical care and a stay. The girls got the rest, no men in there. It's a hard life wherever you go.

At the time, Edinboro had a ratio of 6.5 coeds to every male student. Promiscuity reigned, so did pregnancies. The rate of report, pregnancies; 3.2 per day. Every Friday around 5 PM, a bus, paid for, by whom I don't know; loaded with pregnant coed girls for a trip to the abortion clinics in New York city. Promiscuity has its consequences.

Perhaps the basement of the dorm was not such a bad place to be after all. It made for some funny moments and quick get to know you friendships, in mass. During the course of my stay as a cellar dweller, I met people, I most likely would have had to wait to meet, during the course of a student's tenure on Campus; adjustable by nature; I grew up in an orphanage. Sharing space with other boys was commonplace to me.

A friend of mine from my hometown of Ligonier, Pa. (Barry Wright), living in the cellar with the rest of us, also a gregarious guy we met, Jack Richardson, from Fairview, Pa., there was one other guy in our section of the bivouac, his name was Joe Kish, a Hungarian boy from Pittsburgh: soft spoken, with a shy personality and a good heart. The four of us would form a bond that would get us through those early days at Edinboro State College. There was another group of guys we gravitated too. They all went to Youghiogheny High school near West Newton, South Huntington and Smithton, Pa. These small communities formed Yough High School confidential.

The cellar dwellers were invited to form a softball team; play in the fall semester tournament. A challenge we confidently accepted when we weren't out to save the world. New kids on the block, full of beer and vinegar. Early stages, pre hippies, wanna Be's.

There was Don Pezze', Greg Tekavec, Mark Genemore, and John Mooney, a couple others, the dynamic force representing Yough. We meshed well with these guys; we formed the team that would be known as "The Cellar Dwellers." A formidable unit was now in place, we meant business, not a token entry into the games. Winning was the only thing I knew when it came to competing. No participation trophy for us, steal your face. We needed a couple more guy's to make the nine of us imposing freshmen. I can't forget about our left fielder "Fast Eddie," a sex addict of enigmatic proportions, no self-control, or awareness.

The Cellar Dwellers were making good progress,

working our way through the competition to the champi-
onship game. We, an all-freshman team living in the basement of Schaeffer Hall; were now playing a team of seniors,
all from Fraternities for the softball fall tournament title.
The game was nip and tuck all the way, looking like we
might pull off the upset, these same Greeks won the tournament last year. The game played in a large open field at
the corner of 6 N and the road that ran past the east end
of Edinboro campus. Across the street was a row of houses
running along the edge of campus on the other side of the
street, locals live there.

The game tied up, 7 to 7, we took the field when the
seniors came to bat, last inning. It looked as though the
game would go into extra innings. We had them setup like
a Bolling pin with two outs, it would be extra innings. Our
confidence elevated, hanging with these guys, the pressure
was all on them. We weren't expected to be in the champi-
onship game; they were, all smiles putting the compress on
these cocky guys.

There were two outs with a runner on second base,
scoring position. Just needed one more out to push the
game into extra innings. Those seniors were feeling the
pressure, the fear of losing, their butts   tighten up, they
couldn't walk the talk. The Cellar Dweller freshmen were
about to embarrass them. No one could have predicted
what would happen next.

Fast Eddie our left fielder, fortunately through the en-
tirety of the game, his presence was of no consequence, till
now. One more out, we would be at bat; a chance to go
ahead, win the game, Champs.

While the action was taking place, at the house next to
the left field, right across the street, a family   returning
from the IGA (grocery store) loaded down with groceries.

Parked in their driveway, hatchback up, they began carrying their food into the house.

The next pitch was a soft loop into leftfield, gonna drop right were our left fielder fast Eddie positioned himself; like a monument in place, waiting for a big can of corn, it was going to drop right into his mitt; too easy. If only it would have been a line drive with no time to be distracted from making the catch. We all watched in slow motion, the oohs and awes coming from the spectators watching the game, freeze frame; styling and profiling; we got this!

We all watched Fast Eddie, noticing the sixteen-year-old girl removing bags of groceries from the hatch back of her family car, drop his glove; run across the road to hit on this girl, surprising her and everyone else. In what seemed like slow motion, watching the fly ball land in the very spot Fast Eddie was standing. Didn't have to take a step away from that location, the ball landed on his grassy footprints without rolling, it was planted in that impression. The runner on second base scored, no one on the Cellar Dwellers was able to get to the ball on time to throw to home plate; preventing the score for the last out. We lost! Yes, we lost the game. A bond formed between us; this bond would have lasting values. That day, we really won in the game of life. Fast Eddie, he's still running.

Living in the cellar was not bad. The ping pong tables, and the pool tables were right there with us and the vending machines and the many ways one could cheat the machine. You know, put the money in, watch the product rotate on the pig tail rotator till it reached the end; dropping into the holding area for the buyer to retrieve. The one I can't forget, is the small hole someone drilled into the middle of the plexiglass; using a hanger to knock the chips or cookies into the drop slot.

In the evenings, when we all gathered around into big social groups, the comradery built amongst us was Americana. In those days we lived life vicariously through the precious freedoms of the constitution; our countries founders afforded us without hesitation, though privately, malcontents spoke differently. The early seventies in America was a time when it seemed every day, our lives would be enhanced by new revelations of a society advancing technically and culturally into the future; moving at a dizzying pace, were worlds collide.

No one could know it really was the beginning of the end of those great freedoms we lived by until the 21st century came upon us. Threats to our freedoms disguised as "what's good for us." By those who say they know better. A deceptive dominance, weak minded indoctrinated bored secular citizens bought into, in mass. Freedom, who wants freedom, give them free things instead, they are too stupid to know better. You don't need no stinking freedom. Shut up and sit down.

Six weeks into our residency in the Cellar of Schaeffer Hall, as fate would have it, me, Jack Richardson, Barry Wright and Joe Kish happened to be back at our bunks after lunch in the Cellar when Mr. Odessa, Edinboro's corrupt housing director walked in. He approached us with an offer we couldn't refuse. An apartment in Green Oaks apartments became vacant; available, first come first receive (in our case, first approached), timing is everything. It was for the remaining Edinboro semester at $160 each, four students. Short walk to campus, we had a home. Unchained melodies, let the debauchery begin.

The life we lived could be described, atypical for off campus living by true freshmen. Study, what study, aint no studying going on round here, though I was a History major. We had no restraints. Threw parties every weekend, so much beer, in cans, would be consumed to the extent of not being able to see the carpet on the floor for all the empties. We played tricks with cups of water edged on doors, tickling Barry's nose while he was asleep, putting shaving cream in his palm. Watching Barry smack himself in the face with the shaving cream all over his catalog beard. Unrelenting juvenile stuff. Me and Barry were 19, Jack and Joe 18. Good fun, we weren't out knocking off gas stations or rolling elderly ladies. Just having fun, the collegiate process.

At our first party, Jack and a former female high school classmate from Fairview, arriving at the party, didn't have any love or romance in their relationship, just did things together in a peculiar way. This girl was well put together and a smart ass. A rich girl from Fairview. During the course of the boisterous party, Jack and his Fairview buddy friend went into his bedroom, he shared with Joe Kish, in the living room enjoying the party with the rest of us. Amongst the guests, a happified guy I met the spring before, just before classes ended for the second semester of 1970/71 school year. We met at an off-campus party. Steve went to Thomas and Jefferson High School in Pittsburgh. Now he's in our living room; drunk.

He was the quintessential hippie of our time, you know, the really long dark hair. The John Lennon approach, though he was funny, no threat to anyone but himself; likeable! As the party progressed, Jack with his Fairview girlfriend were out of sight in the bedroom. There goes Steve in his youth and drunkenness stalking the living room reaching out; kissing any old girl he wanted. Imposing his way around the living room to the opening leading to our bedrooms and the bathroom, smooching away.

Just about the time Steve was in the opening by the bedrooms, out of Jacks bedroom comes the girlfriend from Fairview, after polishing Jack's nob. Steve sees her, reaches out, hugs her, landing a solid lip plant on her glossy lips. Out from the bedroom comes Jack, still zipping up his pants, tightening his belt. See's what Steve just did, slaps Steve on the shoulder, Steve see's Jack finishing putting his pants back on, Jack says, "hey man, you just kissed my dick!" Steve loses it! Starts frantically wiping his mouth with his sleeve, spitting everywhere, runs over to the kitchen sink, wash his mouth, water slapping everywhere.

It was a classic moment, especially for the girls who did not appreciate Steve stealing kisses from them. The table has been set for things to come. This is a story for the times it happened (1973), written with as much brutal truth a memory can muster in an effort to get it right, as it was. Return to the scene of what happened. Put on your traveling shoes, the journey begins; a look back at, indelible 1973. Prudes need not apply.

CHAPTER TWO

The following school year of 1972/73, lack of funds, I decided not to enroll for classes, though remain in Edinboro. It was the best place in the world for me to put life on hold, till I could make my way into a future I could hold onto. Growing up Orphan; I was promised a hardship scholarship along with other assistance to continue a college degree in History. It was all talk, more said than done. Nothing was ever presented to me; I would be on my own. Just as well, I could have squandered it. At the time, graduating from high school, I didn't have a reliable safety net I could retreat to; one that wouldn't hold my failures against me. I had to outlive my inferiority complex I wrestled with, growing up orphan, like a Rock.

The summer of 1972, I learned how to approach the hiring system of big corporations of that era. Be the most aggressive person for the opportunity. That, always in any era holds true. Times and methods have changed. In 1972, one had to find their way to the physical person, the person in charge of hiring every new hire; no gauntlet to hurdle on your way to that person. Today, we know them as Human Resources, not as navigable as one person. In 1972, if I could penetrate my way past the secretary to the man (person in charge of hiring), in this case, I could open my mind to him, show him, though I am young, inexperienced, I am growing, a thinker, the future; will my way to being hired. It was him and me. Mano e mano, soul to soul, sitting in a room a desk away from each other. I touched him.

I started as a Broke man cutter, managing a huge paper cutting machine. Cut three pallets at a time of huge sheets of paper. A position of a master, I was far from approaching, the challenge bigger than I could dedicate myself to. Too much too soon, the positive impression I made at hiring, won me this prestige. I had a chance to be the man in that department at 19, out of nowhere. I wasn't serious enough to take it on. I wanted money, pay for my fun times. This boy just wants to have fun. When September rolled round. I became a rolling stone. Wasn't ready to dedicate myself to thirty years with Hammermill Paper Company, had to keep on moving forward to what comes next, the seeker.

In the process of finding another place to live, I crossed paths in town with my Cellar Dweller teammates from Yough High School. We hadn't seen each other since I moved out of the basement into Green Oaks apartments. Going my own way; though we probably did have times when we saw each other on campus between classes, passing like ships in the night. Not often enough that we got together for a smoking good time. Edinboro State College at the time had an enrollment of 8000 students on Campus.

After 1979, many Steel Mills in western Pennsylvania closed for good; changing the landscape of the region, the decline of civilization in western Pennsylvania, the enrollment dropped substantially; in the hurt locker. Consequently, western Pennsylvania lives where scattered across the country seeking employment and a better life.

Edinboro was a bustling place; a former state teachers college in Pennsylvania, with the largest budget, art education, producing teachers. Perhaps that is why so many eccentrics went to school there, why the ratio of women to men was extreme. I was always on the move. Not seeing these guys often enough in the course of a school year made me forget they were at Edinboro. Now we were back where we belong, together again.

They were excited, signing a lease with an apartment complex at the southern edge of campus just off Darrow Road. We referred to this complex as the "Townhouses." Three bedrooms, six students, two to a bedroom, one and a half bath. A living room and dining room split by the kitchen and a basement storing area marked off with chicken wire.

A place to put a bicycle and other items needing storage. Big enough for raucous parties. These guys were amped up, they needed two more roommates, "How would I like to be one of them?" Inviting me to reside with them in Angus 39. All townhouse buildings had names associated with the countries of the United Kingdom, "Edinboro Fighting Scots." The offer was perfect, I agreed to be their 5th roommate, they had to find another, or management of the complex would insert a lone student they chose to live with us.

That's the way it was, dealing with college students in 1972. As it was, we had an uninvited guest living with us. He didn't know what to make of us, creating his own retreat. What no one knew from the outset, we would be the place for parties in the Townhouses. Every day is a winding road, a new revelation on the way to a destination unknown. We took the blinders off, plowing ahead.

Onorato's pizza hired me to be a delivery driver. Everywhere I delivered a pizza, I had to drink a beer, smoke some weed before I could move to the next delivery doing it all over again till I return to Onorato's for another delivery. Onorato's had been around for some time; the pizza was very good, so was business. What my roommates liked about me working there was the call-in pizza's that were not picked up. At the end of work every night, I would always come home with a large pizza, sometimes two of them. I think it was my roommates calling in the Pizza's that were not picked up. They knew the hustle; I fulfilled the routine, Amore'.

We were a band of roving nomads. Our theme song was Led Zeppelins "stairway to Heaven," when we weren't listening to "30 days in the Hole" by Humble Pie, or the band Spirit, Uriah Heep "Demons and Wizards." Captivated by our place in time and space.

Not far across the New York State line was a college called Fredonia State College, part of the New York State University system, I came across Fredonia by accident. Driving to Buffalo New York to see my girlfriend in Williamsburg I met at a large bar named "Uncle Sam's," and the Voelker's of Voelker's lanes, when I heard a loud repetitive flap noise coming from my right front wheel well.

When I stopped my 1966 Dodge Coronet, the tear in the tire was not evident upon visual inspection. Baffling. Start, move, a little faster, the more it flopped in the wheel well, louder. Stop again, can't identify the problem, take off again. Flop, flop, slowly I drove the car into downtown Fredonia looking for answers.

Entered a Burger King inquiring information, who could help fix my tire on a Sunday night in Fredonia, New York. That is when Mike Petraglia from Long Island walked in, listening to my dilemma offered me a place to sleep in his co-ed dormitory, which I though was cool. Nice to meet you. The setup in this dorm was much like an apartment. There was a floor community room, like a living room. Had a TV and couches, a place I could sleep, oh yes, there were beautiful co-eds sharing the floor with the guys, brilliant idea.

The next day, at the auto repair shop, the mechanic pointed out what the problem with the tire was. I replaced it with another cheap retread, thanked Mike for his help, deciding we would be friends. I would be back to check out the makings of life in Fredonia, New York. It was summertime, when I returned with friends, we enjoyed the Fredonia bar scene. That small college town was almost a mirror image of what Edinboro was at that time. Twins from different states. Another place I could disappear too.

It was early November 1972, I suggested to my Angus 39 roommates we ought to drive up to Fredonia Friday night. Show off Fredonia to my buddies, let one rip for the evening, a place for us to thunder. We took over a bar, our presence was profound; we had everyone in the joint dancing and jumping up and down in unison; raving before people knew the term. I like beer, it makes me a jolly fellow. They had no idea we were not students from Fredonia state. We took the place over, an impression what our parties at Angus 39 metastasized into. In all the excitement, I lost my wristwatch during all the raving as it sailed through the air like a hockey puck.

Dave Gromacki from Erie, and I were left behind. I do not recall who did the driving to Fredonia. We tried hitchhiking back to Edinboro though late-night travel in that neck of the woods was defeating. We ended up sleeping in the lobby of an old hotel at the outskirts of town. Front door was unlocked, we went in, saw no one there to pay for a room; we took up sleep on the couches. Dave used the pay phone to call his brother in Erie. He arrived as the sun broke the horizon that morning, breaking the darkness into light.

The end of semester closing in on us, more changes would have to be made for the next semester. My roommates decided they would be moving to another place, I had to figure out what my next move would be. I certainly didn't think it would be decided by a dream I melted into. My next-door neighbor from Angus 38, John Mark Donahue from Meadville, Pa. was in our apartment more than he was in his; only sleeping there. He and I had met by virtue of being neighbors. Mark sported a happy personality, liked to laugh, we took him in; one of us.

Not much time left before everyone would be vacating the premises going back to their families and hometowns for the Christmas Season. Christmas was never a time I looked forward too. It was two days after Christmas, my mother died in 1958, Christmas would always be a reminder of that heartache. I didn't have a place to go to for Christmas though my brother Sal was living in Ligonier, I could look to him for lodging. An oasis for respite, taking chances; never fearing the outcome.

One-night friends came over to Angus 39, people stopping by, usually with weed for sale, some goodies in the way of pills or psychedelics. This particular visit, I was offered little green barrel shaped pills known as soapers. They were called downers because they were not uppers. If one took too many, they made the person sleepy, the party for them would be over. Back then, we had different designer drugs of the time. I wouldn't take anything unless I saw the supplier take it first or I trusted the person distributing the high. Maliciousness not the norm in that era. I don't know how the young people of current generation protect themselves from badly made designer drugs. It's like Russian Roulette.

The soapers were just the right amount for me, have esthetically pleasing dreams all night long. Next morning, my sleep was interrupted by my neighbor Mark Donahue. Still in bed, having a wonderful dream about being in Hawaii. I was in the surf at Waikiki Beach in Honolulu,

Hawaii. Three hula girls calling my name from the beach, clamoring for me to come out of the water, be with them.

They were all gorgeous in their grass skirts, hips swaying, they wanted me. In return, I wanted them to join me in the waves. The bantering going back and forth when Mark Donahue came into my bedroom, waking me up. Ideas come from the strangest of places, destiny makers.

My mind went straight from the dream to the sound of Mark's voice. Before he could say another word, sitting up in bed, fixated by the dream, I started telling him about it. When I was finished, I said, "I'm going to Hawaii!" Mark said, "I'm going with you!" From there on I would put together a plan for us to travel to Florida, acquire jobs through the winter. When we had enough money, we would travel to California, do it all over again; till we had the desired amount of money making the plane ride to Honolulu, setting up our new lives in Hawaii. I thought that would be my future, I applied myself, make it happen. A natural formula determined by a faith; I would learn to master.

Mark liked my idea so much; he recruited two more guys from Meadville to join us on this big adventure. Jerry, a real stoner and his equal; Gator, legally blind, saddled with hearing aids. This was going to be interesting trip to Florida. We would do it in my 1966 Dodge Coronet with bucket seats, a 318 cubic motor, it had guts! Be careful what you wish for, you just might get it. Then what?

First, I would go back to my hometown, Ligonier, regroup, prepare myself for the journey that would kick start my future, keeping the rabbit in front of me, something to chase, time moves on. I will always have something in my life to chase. When the chase is over, so will I be. Keep moving! Everyone has to have a reason to be. Reach beyond your reach, the rewards embrace you. Find out who you are?

My brother Sal and Lee Skinner, graduated in the same Ligonier Valley senior class. They were living in a cabin on Laurel Mountain overlooking Lynn Run State Park; with the cabins owner, Frank Chianese a short order cook in Johnstown. Frank was a good guy though he was a lush, alcohol got the best of him. Frank welcomed me to stay at his cabin prior to my trip south to Florida. The month of January 1973 would set the tone for the rest of that glorious year.

There were two cats in the yard (Emo & Mod), life used to be so hard, now everything is easy living at the cabin, though Frank refused to let them inside with the heat. These two cats had to be tough to endure winter on Laurel Mountain. They would often huddle together in the dried-out flower trough outside the Kitchen window. Snow collecting on their fur. They kept the rodent problem under control. When Lee & Sal could, they worked together on custom wood projects Lee contracted to customers.

The drive to the cabin off Lynn Run was a long and winding road; dirt and gravel surface, add snow and ice, even more difficult to traverse. The mount top was spooky up there at nighttime, though it seemed we always had company, the distance to the summit worth it. Back then, all television was rabbit ear antenna. Up on the mountain top, we had really good reception. So good we were able to pick up the UHF stations clearly, down below, they came in fuzzy. Rustic living.

It was on one of those UHF network stations we watched Leon Russell and the Shelter people recorded live in a Los Angeles recording studio. I remember thinking how it felt listening to Leon Russell; his fantastic song writing; his dexterity on piano, not to mention the pulsating action taking place between the musicians. It was then I decided it was Leon Russell I like the most. I loved to Rock & Roll, Leon was at the pinnacle of that sound and vibe in the music business of the day. The organizer of the "Mad Dogs and Englishman" tour of 1970, salvaging Joe Cockers career. Leon, master of space and time.

This was also the year of the Immaculate Reception, part of NFL and Pittsburgh Steeler folklore between the Steelers and the Oakland Raiders. When Franco Harris made the incredible catch deflected by Oaklands Jack Tatum off a pass from Terry Bradshaw to French Fuqua, next to no time left in the game. Allowing Franco to return the ball to the end zone giving the Steelers a most improbable victory for the ages. Greatest play in NFL history. We watched the game in the cabin on a small 15-inch color Television, a reflection of our past. Penn States John Cappelletti won college football's 1973 Heisman Trophy for his dying brother Joey.

The following week my brother Sal went to Pittsburgh, attending the now famous game between the Steelers and the undefeated Miami Dolphins. Miami's punter Larry Siebel, noticed all the Steeler defenders on the punt, turned their backs to him; running to the ball to block for the receiver. Larry decided not to punt, run the ball for a long gain, first down, score.

Consequently, assuring that Miami would be going to the Super Bowl against over the hill Gang, Washington Redskins. To this day, the only team in the modern era to go undefeated. When we weren't in the cabin, more like a hunting lodge with two bunk rooms, we were at Hosa's bar watching the football games. It was a cozy place we could skate the state laws. Drink after hours when Tom locked the door, turned on the closed sign, lights off, blinds closed, as you were, free to be.

The private party would resume, joints floating around, it was a time of great freedom. No paranoia, young people enjoying life by our own rules, troubling no one with our frisky behavior. Historically, there are those pontificators who believe the year 1973 was the last free era, when freedom would be prevalent in United States. 1973 was to the east coast what 1967 was to the west coast, particularly San Francisco. As the decades passed on, technology gained control over the freedoms populations would enjoy, in 1973, believing in a higher power, free to express ourselves, be happy. Now a dying breed.

Soon, I would be driving to Meadville, pick up Mark, Jerry and Gator for our trip southbound to Florida. I could not have known what I was wishing for, throwing caution to the wind. When the last weekend of January arrived, like planned, drive to Meadville; pick up my travel buddies, beginning an adventure beyond expectations; never to be forgotten. We all returned to Ligonier from Meadville, having a few days before we set out for our grand scheme, move to Hawaii.

Mark suggested we drive into Pittsburgh, see if we could find friends from Meadville attending a concert in downtown Pittsburgh. Driving along Liberty avenue, Mark saw his friends and a girl I knew, Penny, from Meadville. The concert they attended was over. Penny a precocious young women I was intrigued with. She would not be going to Florida with us. We shouted out to her and the others, pulled over to let them into the car. We drove back to Lynn Run state park, were the cabin on the mountain, Rector; was located.

After a night on the couch with Penny, a room full of people, I had the worst case of the blue balls I ever experienced. Too modest to go the distance under the spotlight.

18

Next morning, I took Penny and the others with her back to Meadville. It was a few days later, the four of us headed south to Florida by way of Northern Virginia. During my Christmas stay in Ligonier, I ran into a girlfriend buddy I graduated high school with, home for the Christmas holidays. She was living near Washington, D.C. in northern Virginia, beginning her career working for a Bank.

After a wild night of dancing in a Georgetown nightclub, we spent the night at Barbs apartment with her roommates. The next day, we left our young ladies behind, Barb considered going with us till I made her come to her senses. Traveling down interstate 95, it felt like we were going to New Orleans with Arlo Guthrie while Roberta Flack was killing us softly with someone else's song. Charlie Rich, stuck behind closed doors with the most beautiful girl in the world. Tunes on the radio of the day playing over and over again, the soundtrack of our trip.

CHAPTER THREE

We continued south on Interstate 95. Stopped at a fast-food drive-in near Savannah, Georgia, the kind where the girl arrives on roller skates, takes your order. The all-day drive and ride took the steam out of us. After we ate, I drove past Jacksonville until we made it to Melbourne, Florida where we slept on the beach for the night, listening to soothing sounds of waves breaking.

None of us had ever been to Florida, this would be the next best thing to being in Hawaii, our ultimate destination. Amazing that an inexperienced group like us really believed in our plan, make it to Florida without a net. Work, earn enough money, drive to California, do it all over again, then make our way to Hawaii.

The next day, early morning sun shining, rolling away the dew, we wiped the sea salt and body grease off our faces. Jubilant for the first time in our lives, all of us were in Florida, felt like Christmas morning when the sun came up. I have to say, the first time was a spiritual sensation for me, not sure how it affected the other guys. We were young, happy to be alive pursuing a dream, pointed in a direction.

Isn't that what life is all about, dynamic experiences with breath-taking feelings. A new sensation, attacking an idea, making it work. Not the same honorable dream as raising a family; those who's souls are built for it, it's not for everyone, though mightily essential. God decides what's too many. Time would be on our side to decide. Make the changes, lean into life, always reaching beyond our reach. If you can't touch it, scratch it!

Needing gas, stopped at a Shell station, filled up the gas tank, went inside for drinks, snacks, restroom. Before I could get the car out of the Shell station, a white-haired man, perhaps in his eighties backing up his auto, dinged my car parked next to the pumps. He gets out of his car take the measure of what happened; actually, standing there scratching his head, not understanding how it happened. I thought, well this is the land of retirement, had to be aware of the old timers behind the wheel. Assessing the dimple in the bumper; considered it nothing to concern myself, told him not to worry, we both left the Shell station in opposite directions.

The boys from Meadville had a good friend from Meadville living in Orlando; we decided to go there, look him up, see if he could provide us with a place to stay, temporary sanctuary. Arriving in Orlando at an address that would be our derstination, only to find the guy from Meadville was not home. His where abouts unknown. The neighbor we talked with said he hadn't been around for weeks. We left, did some local sightseeing, returning later, check on his return home. Still not there! What to do? We asked a neighbor if there were any low rent places nearby, we could stay for a couple nights. We were guided to a Boarding House at North Magnolia and Hillcrest street.

Upon arrival, we found some of the guests lying about, drinking beer, smoking pot. The only person missing was Panama Red. All living on the edge of surviving. We asked what the cost for a room was for a night. Ten dollars a week for a small room with shared bathrooms. It was a motley crew of struggling people, we fit right in. There were three young girls in their early twenties, they came to Florida. Help one of the girls who was pregnant, have her baby out of sight from all who knew them in Columbus, Ohio. Not quite there yet in 1973.

My impression of these three girls was positive. They

were clean cut educated girls wanting to help one of their loving friends get past this experience in her life.

Not wanting an abortion, careful consideration; offering the baby up for adoption, have a chance at life. A soul waiting to enter the world in the form of a newborn baby. Owning up to the responsibility of ones decisions and actions. Give the unborn a chance at life like those who get live it, love will endure. Eventually we all die. After this experience of humanity for however long it is. The challenge; don't take it away.

There was a guy from Illinois, he was on his own sojourn looking for a new life in Florida. He was not a threat to anyone but himself, his reckless behavior for drugs and pot, his master. There were others staying there, though we would have to wait for them to come back to the house. After their day was done picking oranges in the fields as temps; an opportunity that was presented to us. At this time, we were not taking. The first night would be all we needed, should we to stay, or should we go? Miami calling.

The rest of the boarders back at the house, partying ramped up. Running low on weed, the guy from Illinois says he knows where to go, Eaola Park, pick up some smoke, perhaps other party favors as well. Offered us to go along with him. My sixth sense told me this public park could be a trap, by the local authorities. I convinced the other guys not to go with him. The law back then had an aggressive attitude towards pot. Besides, we were enjoying ourselves with the girls from Ohio. Some of the other boarders took that chance, went along with this reckless guy from Illinois.

Later in the evening they came back to the house empty handed with a story of what transpired at Eaola Park. Turns out, the park was a breeding ground for undercover narcotics cops. The guy from Illinois was busted, now in the Orlando city jail. It took a moment to realize how fortunate those of us were; not going along. Though I had never been to Orlando, Florida before this time, my intuition was correct, I always trust my instincts. When I don't, it could be bad news for me. Not this time! This was a wakeup call for all of us, we were in unchartered territory. It would be wise to move on from Orlando, but not before we spend a day at the newly opened Disney World, on the bucket list, now the chuck it list.

When we were in the park, preparing to ride the overhead rail across the expanse of the park, just the look of us made employees tell us to not smoke weed on the monorail; the people in the towers would be watching, we could get kicked out of the park. We did it anyway, no one noticed. Rule breakers! Later after we left, packed up in the car, got on interstate 4 east towards I 95 south, slept at a rest stop for the night. We dodged a bullet the night before, our ramble through the state of Florida almost ended before we could embrace it.

In the morning, back on the road again, interstate 95, deciding to drive all the way to south Florida, deep into the sunshine we would go. Take advantage of the brilliant weather, its ever warm feeling the further south we went. Clueless about what we would do once we arrive at our unknown destination. Blowing in the wind, arriving at Hollywood, Florida, now in the hands of fate. Nobody told me it would be this way.

The weather was a balmy 72 degrees, overcast, though we left life below zero temperatures, ice road truckers, we were in Shangri-La. Giddy at the prospect of swimming in the Atlantic ocean. We better hit the surf. Back then, unlike now, one could ride along the beach in Hollywood,

Florida. Park the car right there at the edge of the sand, swim in the ocean. Not anymore, it's blocked off from thru travel via cars; my mind is going through them changes.

Experienced swimming in the ocean from my youthful visits to my Uncles home in New Jersey, in 1967. I knew how to ride the waves, swim with strong currents, as I had at Wildwood Beach, New Jersey in the 1960's. For the other three guys, it would be their first time in the ocean, first time anywhere.

No fear, heading into what was a high surf with an undertow, something I was used too, did my playful frolic of body surfing the waves. Having my fill, left the water for a rest on the beach, dry off. While I was in the ocean, the other's guys watched me having fun, not sure how to go about it themselves, hesitating till they saw me emerge safely from the Atlantic ocean. Must be OK; Mark and Gator thought, Jerry declined to enter the water. I turned my attention away from Mark, he moved towards the water's edge. Jerry and Gator momentarily got my attention, I looked away.

Scanning the surf to see what happened to Mark, was he adjusting to the pull of the undertow, the high surf, pulling him down into a washing machine roll as it often does when the timing is off on a body surf. At first, I couldn't locate him, my gaze became more concerning, I saw Mark drifting, listing further out to sea, standing on his toes to keep his head above water, his arms spread out in T-formation.

Immediately, I knew he was in trouble, if I could not get to him, he would surely be sucked out to sea, drown. I won't let that happen. Like a lifeguard would, I ran into the water diving into the breaking surf, swimming against the strong current, I made my way to Mark who was now in panic duress. We were in deeper water, his feet no longer on the bottom, his arms stretched out on the surface of the ocean for buoyancy. Reaching for Mark, hooking one of his arms with mine, locking him in.

I began to swim towards the beach, towing Mark with me, his body flattened out, he did not fight me like many people are prone to do when they face drowning. Got him into shallow water, helping him the rest of the way onto the beach, he was exhausted, in a mild state of shock, still alive; not gonna make the nightly news.

Relieved he was safe, I looked to Jerry, who had a horrified look on his face, looking past me towards the surf. No Gator on the beach, reacting to Jerry's eyes, I turned looking out to the ocean. Just like Mark, I could see Gator being sucked out into the deeper water, instant replay. No time to think, I ran into the water again, dove into the surf swimming as fast as I could against the rip tide to reach Gator who was legally blind, dependent on hearing aids, now lost at sea.

He was further out than Mark was, daunting as it was, I had to go get him. There was no one else on the beach. I could not stand by, watch Gator drown. Again, without hesitation, no consideration for my own safety, instinctively put my life on the line, came naturally to me. It would have been hard to live with myself had I not. I'm the reason these guys are here in Florida. After this day, they would continue to be my responsibility, they live.

Gator was floating, arms stretched out, I hooked one of them, muscled Gator next to me. I began to swim back to the beach, like Mark, he did not fight me, he knew I was there to help him. Once we were back on the sandy beach, I was able to relax knowing twice we had averted tragedies. I didn't have time to think about the danger. I was mentally fatigued, more so than what it took out of me physically. I thanked God for giving me the strength and courage to be there for Mark and Gator. Didn't see that coming.

Up against it, saving someone's life was not something I ever anticipated happening. One never knows what experiences are waiting. When life looks like easy street, there could be danger at your door. Unfortunately, later in life, John Mark Donahue informed me in May of 2022 while visiting with him in Meadville, Pa.; many years later, Gator passed away by drowning, ironic. Almost happened February 1973. He still had more time.

After a rest period on the beach, regaining our composure, deciding to get back in the car, drive a little further south, find a place we could stay for the night. While traveling down Florida's A1A we noticed this thin looking red headed guy with a quizzical look on his face, hitchhiking. I asked the other guys, "what do ya think, should we pick him up, he might be able to give us a place to stay for the night."

"Yeah, pick him up." What a decision this would turn out to be, a crap shoot. He gets in the back seat full of chatter, happy we picked him up. Getting to know him, turns out he was from our part of the world, Pittsburgh. He moved to Hollywood, Florida staying just down the road in an efficiency his girlfriend paid for, he the honored guest.

This guy was in art school; his girlfriend welcomed him to stay in her efficiency while he gave her pleasure. We wanted to smoke some weed; we had none left. He said, "take me home, I will get you stoned, you can have a place to stay for the night." Wow, we hit the jackpot, or so we thought. Once we made it to the efficiency, like he said, pulled out some smoke. We commenced to relax, a place for the night, we were getting stoned. Things were about to get interesting, so much so, the charts could not measure it. 1973 was like being on a slow-moving river, the rapids getting faster and faster, headed for the edge of a waterfall.

While we were enjoying the comfort of a safe place to be, toking away, enthusiastic about our good fortune, there was a knock on the door. Unannounced, who could this be? The lanky red headed guy opens the door, to all's relief, he knew the guy, he did not come empty handed. Standing there before us, it looked as though he brought a bouquet of flowers for us; though our presence was as much a surprise to him as he was to us. They were yellow flowers, having a shape like tulips, with deep purple veins inside the flowers. Said they were plants to trip by "Belladonna plants." Yes, like an acid (LSD) trip. Never heard of this before. Could he be out to trick all of us, pilfer our limited cash reserves?

He seemed sincere, since they were only one dollar a flower, why not take a chance. This was an era when firsts were happening all the time. Be afraid to take chances and miss out, take chances, be rewarded, or the fool. What to do? I was mentally exhausted from the events at Hollywood beach, Jerry was lax in his decision making, we each bought one flower, while Mark and Gator were gung-ho, they bought and ate two flowers each.

Flowers consumed, home from work, enter the red headed guy's girlfriend; she was not impressed her boy toy brought us to her dwelling. The tension in the air was palpitating. We did not have to be told we were not welcome. No worries, we tasted we got wasted, ate the plants, now it was time we were not there anymore; resume finding a place for the night. I had the most money of the four of us, deciding I would pay for a motel room, accommodate the four of us comfortably. Driving along the waterfront, feeling like contenders, I picked out a quaint beachfront motel for the night in Hollywood.

In the short time it took to find this motel, Mark and Gator, were losing coherency, the two plants they consumed were doing exactly what the stranger said they would do. Mark and Gator left me and Jerry for the outer limits, entering the twilight zone. Jerry and I felt nothing, he stayed out of the ocean, also avoided eating two plants. This was Jerry's fortunate son day. Together, our day was long from being over, onto night moves.

On Hollywood beach we came across a mellow looking motel, it struck me, we should stop the search, accept this place as ours for the night, get over the exhausting day, that almost turned tragic. Not quite, still, we were in jeopardy, though we were not astute enough to acknowledge it, when we stopped for the night to get accommodations. Only then did I realize Mark and Gator had left us, in the deep divide, lost in space. They would not be coming home this night, lost lonely boys in the abyss of their minds, stuck in the middle with them.

I left them in the car with Jerry. Entering the charming motel office, the manager was a friendly guy, the owner of the property. He was from the greatest generation that fought World War 2. Trusting me, securing two connecting rooms for the night. Each room had two queen beds and a bathroom. I knew I had a reason for picking this place for the night, perfect. Walked back to the car, keys to the rooms in hand, the manager/owner stood in the doorway of his office, smiling at me. All's well in Hollywood, Florida tonight. Nothing to see here.

I noticed the short grassy courtyard walk to our rooms. A group of elderly people sitting around two tables with large umbrellas above them, mellowing out in the warm evening ocean breeze. I opened the car door, looked in to see what I was up against, there was no way to communicate with Gator and Mark. Jerry in a state of what to do, now we have to walk the courtyard for all to see, to its grassy end, near the old people relaxing in front of their rooms under their awnings. Under a spotlight, all eyes on us. No where to run, nowhere to hide.

Looking at Mark and Gator, knowing I would have to put on my best dancing shoes to fool the old guy standing at the office door, waiting to see who emerged from the car; legit or not. "OK Jerry, you take Mark, help him walk, I'll take Gator, follow me to our rooms at the left side at the back of the courtyard." Mark and Gator at first glance looked intoxicated, they had trouble walking and talking, legs wobbly. I knew better, the old guy watching from the office steps had questions. As we moved, weaved our way through the courtyard holding them up, in jeopardy of losing the room. The owner stepping off the office steps like he might come closer, get a better look, he had that Norman Fell look on his face (what the hell is going on here)?"

Looking to him, weak smile on my face, I said, "They had too much to drink." What we needed to confuse the old guy, keep him guessing, we continued to the rooms. However, the two tables of elderly people or retired people were up and running for their rooms, like their hair was on fire; slamming their doors shut, the zombies are coming. If it wasn't real, I would have thought I was the one tripping.

That is how I imagined they were seeing it. Successful, we had the private sanctuary of these two connecting rooms; ride this mistake out. I shared a room with Gator, Jerry shared a room with Mark.

We would have the responsibility of being their care takers, keep the peace. This was the impossible dream. Mark and Gator were lost in space, we absolutely could not communicate with them. They may well have been ghosts for what communications we thought we were having with them. Now they were poltergeist, scaring the hell out of me and Jerry.

At this point, my hands full with Gator, what ingrained cerebral instincts he had left, we had a failure to communicate. All I wanted to do was go to sleep, mentally and physically muted. I saved two lives today. Certain the fatigue played a part, not getting high from the Belladonna plant I ate. Two crushed Mark and Gator, the two who almost died that day; surviving to go through this nightmare. Death have no mercy! Definitely not their time to be gone.

In a battle of wills with Gator. Encouraging him to lay down, go to sleep. Gator smoking invisible cigarettes, putting them out, invisible ash tray. He had no cigarette in his fingers, he kept on smoking them, one after another, I pleaded with him to go to sleep. Gator with a little help from me, laid down in his bed. All was quiet and still on the cosmic front, good, he is going to sleep. Now I can go to sleep; it did not take long, I was on my way to sleep, checking out the first sheep. I felt something at my feet.

Opened my eyes, there was Gator, standing on the edge of my bed looking down on me with this wild-eyed look. What the hell! I got out of bed, pulled Gator off of it. Tried as I might getting through to him, he kept saying to me, I was a Narc; I turned him into the law. Exasperating as it was, I had to keep my eyes on him. Sleep would have to overcome me if I was to have any sleep at all. This is a manic situation. Everything was fluid at that point.

Gator went in and out of compliancy, then become a

mystery to me all over again. I would dose off, wake up, hear Gator talking with someone. There was no one in the room, Gator was in the bathroom shower, I walked in to see what he was doing in there, who he was communicating with. No one, Gator was in another dimension talking to an invisible rabbit named Harvey. Could have been, who could say not?

Gator puked all over the shower wall, didn't sober him up. In the other room, Jerry watching over Mark, a total mystery to me what was going on in there. Overwhelmed in my side of the rooms. I lost consciousness, fell into a deep slumber, in the morning when I woke, looked to Gators bed, he was not there. Got out of bed, walked into the next room to see Jerry asleep and no Mark. What is coming next? The hopeful expectations they would be sitting outside our doors having tea and crumpets, slap happy with the elderly people they scared the night before.

My first reaction, take a shower, get refreshed, the day in front of us uncertain, where was Mark and Gator? Jerry and I didn't have much to gather up, knew nothing about what happened with Mark under Jerry's watch during the night. Concerned about Gator and Mark, we exited the Motel rooms; didn't get very far from the door when the owner of the motel rushes up to us. Startled by his omnipresence, we froze at the sight of him, expecting to get chewed out, and don't ever come back. I spoke first, asking him if he had seen Mark and Gator. "Yeah," tersely he says, "I seen 'em!"

"The guy with the beard and earing (Gator), he was trying to climb into the window of that room over there when I stopped him, he ran off. The other guy, (Mark), he was on his hands and knees, weeding through the grass with his fingers. I asked him what he was doing?" He said, "I'm looking for my brother."

That is when I last saw him." Our first adventure, what to do? Too inexperienced, immature to manage this situation. We loaded up into the 66 Dodge Coronet, deciding to ride around town, look for them. Grasping for answers, how will this end? Did I save them yesterday only to find them dead today?

They were way beyond any "High" we experienced with anyone in our young hippie lives. Jerry was six days older than me, both 20 headed for 21 in July of 1973. Jerry and I never did find Gator and Mark. We concluded, eventually someone would bring them to the attention of the Law if not by their own doing. The local Police Department would sort things out for them, send Mark and Gator home to their families in Meadville, Pa. Jerry and I moved on without them, we had no other way to go but to chase the dream of working and living in Hawaii; there was nothing else. Not gonna quit, don't know what that is. Then there was two. The journey just beginning.

Don't recall what happened to Gator. He was found by the police, when he recovered, they contacted his family, he went back to Meadville, Pa. on a Greyhound bus thanks to money wired to Western Union. Here's what happened to Mark, what he told me when I caught up with Mark that summer, my return to Edinboro, Pennsylvania. Mark said he hallucinated seeing me in a Cadillac convertible, drive past him as he stood on a street corner, still out of his mind. Said, I just got married, even saw my bride sitting in the front seat of the car with me. All decked out in her white wedding dress, you know, the classic just married sign on the car, the cans being dragged from behind, in his mind, clanging on the street.

Mark said he would plead with my illusion for me to

32

stop, pick him up. He said, I would respond by saying, "stay there, I will be right back," in his mind, I continued driving around a corner. Mark said I must have gone around the block five times; him pleading for me to stop. I would say, "I'll be right back." Of course, this was all a fantasy of his condition; I asked, "What happened next?" He said he walked along the sidewalk in Hollywood, Florida till he came to a big flowery bush. Mark said, in this bush, he saw all of his friends, like Christmas bulbs hanging on the limbs of the bush.

Mark decided, because all his buddies were in the bush, he would stand in the bush, be with them. That was when a policeman approached, asking what Mark what he was doing in that bush? Mark told the Police officer his friends were in the bush, he wanted to be with them, that is why he was standing in the bush. That was all it took. He was taken into custody (not arrested), till he came out of his trip from two Galaxies over. His situation sorted out, a call made home to Meadville, Pa., money wired to Western Union, eventually making his way home, freeing him from his Cosmic Journey.

Meanwhile Jerry and I were just beginning to have our great adventure. Never did see or talk with Gator again, have no idea how he survived his mind-bending trip. Now he's gone, nothing is going to bring him back. Jerry and I decided to make a go of it staying in South Florida, finding a $20 a week room in north Miami, it was 1973! The room had everything we needed, two beds, a bathroom with shower, a little balcony overlooking a dismal neighborhood, a bar next door, with people one step above our social statis. We would have to grow older wiser quickly to survive in these circumstances. Jerry was laid back, couldn't be bothered with details. I would be making all the decisions from now on, handle with care.

Saturday, we decided to go over the bridge to Virginia Key, we got wind of a big waterfront party going on over there. This would be our real first taste of Florida sunshine fun. The scene on Virginia Key, a Woodstock like event.

Hippies, Jesus freaks, Baptist's, pan handlers and the motorcycle club "The Outlaws," and other odd balls and a few legitimates, were all there soaking up the sun and music. Jerry and I split up agreeing to meet later on at my car.

Walking along, a group of Outlaws rode past me to a spot they could all safely leave their motorcycles. One of the bikers, a large man of about six foot eight or more, looked to weigh 350 pounds, face full of black hair, an imposing figure of a man with a beautiful long-legged blond girl on the back of his Harley. I stood back watching him; awed as he got off his huge Harley Davidson motorcycle, looked small with him on it. I found my way beachside. Walking along this magnificent beach of fine white sand, clear skies, emerald water, paradise. Wildwood, New Jersey never looked this good. The ocean water was warm, the big waves slapping the beach silly.

Taking the people in, watching activities along the shoreline, it had the aura of being in a movie. Came upon a black preacher man baptizing people in the surf. As he bellowed out the blessings, he held the people under with the firm grip of his hand, any longer under, he would drown them. The waves crashing over their bodies. It was a spectacle. Casually pacing on down the beach, I came across people lying on their backs looking up towards the sun, horizontal to a beach bush. Not sure what drugs they were on, perhaps LSD or Quaaludes, they were totally out of it, turning to bacon. I was concerned for their eyes. I moved on till I got to the gay end of the beach. I'd gone far enough; I turned back the way I came.

Met two guys doing the same thing Jerry and me were doing, adventurous, adrift in a sea of people, looking for a job opportunity; a place to rest their traveling bones, drifters. One was from Binghamton; New York, the other was a former jockey from Massachusetts, little guy, smaller than me. Together we found Jerry walking along the beach. That is when we split from the other two guys we met, see ya on down the road. Later in the afternoon, we decided it would be a good idea, get off the island, retreat to our north Miami bungalow, where over beers we met two young couples from Indiana staying in our boarding house.

Like us, they were looking for work in the local job market, intent on staying in south Florida, done with Indiana winters, no looking back. Jerry and I bonded with them, they were honest people, comforting in a place where we knew no one, all the ones around us looked dark. During our conversations with the two couples, realizing we were after the same results, come Monday, we would look for work with the girls, the boyfriends already had construction jobs.

Bought a Sunday Miami Herald, marked out perspective job opportunities in the paper, our plan in place. Our attitude, we were going to make this work. Late Monday morning, around 11 AM, four of us loaded up the car, newspaper in hand. We set out for the places marked out as real possibilities for employment. Minimum wage jobs at a factory, searching in an area of north Miami, we should have been cautious about traversing.

None of us familiar with the locale, feeling our way through the process when out of nowhere a police car moves in behind us, puts on the blue lights, pulling us over. Not knowing why, I obliged. One of the officers comes to the driver's side window, looks at my license. Sees I'm from Pennsylvania; asks me what we are doing cruising this neighborhood?

I told him we were looking for addresses, pointing to the ones I marked out with a pen in the job section of the Miami Herald; circled them, all factory job opportunities. He asked me if I knew where we were? "Not really," I replied. "We are looking for work." The officer looks into the back seat, sees the two young ladies from Indiana, says, "do you want your women rapped?" Naively, not comprehending his intent, surprised he would ask me that, I said, "No!"

"Well then, you better get out of this neighborhood if you don't want that to happen!" I understood, we were in no man's land or should I say no women's land, a blighted place on the map. The crude officer handed my license back; turning around, that was it for a job search today. We went back to the boarding house, beer thirty. When in doubt, light one up, have some suds, let the music play on. One thing about music, it makes you feel OK, hit me with music.

The next day while driving around, we observed guys our age playing pickup football game in a local Hialeah public Park. They invited us to join them. Made the mistake of getting high before we met them. Never played football high on pot. My passion not deterred, playing with reckless abandon like I always had; can't change my stripes. We were sore the next day. Jerry wasn't much of an athlete. When we were done playing football, the guys we played, befriended us, inviting Jerry and me to a party in Coral Gables, Florida where the university of Miami is located. As Popeye would say, "Goils."

Jerry and I drifting vagabonds with no particular place to go or be, seekers. Coral Gables felt lonely, being a well-manicured place, people with money and comfort all around us. Feeling out of place though we decided we would attend this party, there were pretty girls there, always happy to meet the Florida girls. One day I would Marry one. Later that evening, we made our way over to the address we were givin for the party. Surprisingly, we were greeted as honored guests, perhaps because we were from Pennsylvania, visitors, or just my imagination running away with me.

The guys inviting us were not kidding, the girls at the party were friendly and gorgeous. Once we entered the party, we were handed a little orange round barrel shaped pill. "Take it," our lovely host said, it's Orange Sunshine." Looked like a small piece of tasty candy, I popped it into my mouth, settling back for the ride. Jerry melted into a sandbag on the floor staying in his own world throughout the party. I made my way around the apartment socializing with the other guests. Thanking the guys inviting us, the LSD took hold of me, potent, though surprised how clean it was; someone asked me my name?

The LSD crowding my mind, all I could say, "I don't have a name, you can call me horse." Laughter erupted; I exited the room collecting myself, escaping the attention. The Roller Coaster took off. At one point, I was teetering on the edge, not sure if I could go higher without losing my handle on this trip. Watched people flashing water sticks with different colors, floating liquid in them, deciding I needed some fresh air. Went out into the parking lot were other people gathered. Moving away from them, fighting to keep control of my mind, I moved out of the light, into a dark spot under a willow tree.

An exotic car with tinted windows pulls up next to me, the glass comes down, the driver, a well-dressed black guy asks me, "is there a party going on in this building?" All the others moved inside by the time this happened. Not knowing if this guy was legit, an invite, my senses heightened, instinctively I said, "Party, what party, I don't know about no party." He shook his head driving off. I looked for cover inside. Don't remember much about the rest of the night. Strangers in a strange land. We survived, returning in the morning to our boarding house in north Miami. Reach or retreat, how to experience?

Where our boarding house was to everything worthwhile in Miami, deciding we would go back to Orlando once our weeks' worth of rent was up; give it another look, perhaps things would be different this time around. We knew about the $10 a week boarding house with the wholesome girls from Columbus, Ohio. In 1973, Orlando had a funky energy about it, a small city in transition beginning Orlando's surge into the noticeable spotlight; thanks to Walt Disney and the new world his vision built around Orlando.

The growth brought in hustlers, scammers, shiftless people out to trick people, also vagrants and drug dealers hotly pursued by the local authorities with a fervor. A transient society, one would have to have their wits about them, keep from being sucked into a bad deal. Everyone's on the take, opportunities for a quick buck and a chance to make a stupid decision. People were flooding in everyday from all over the country. Jerry and I happened to be two more, young and unsuspecting. We would need guardian Angels treading our way around Orlando, Florida in February of1973. It had a wild west feeling to it, the human gold rush, the beginning of what we know it to be now, these days and times.

Back in Orlando, at the boarding house at North Magnolia and Hillcrest street, staying there though offsite management unaware Jerry and I came back. We were sheltered by the people who were paying to live there. They liked partying with us, we were harmless to them. I always brought a sense of humor with me; people liked my presence. Besides the girls from Ohio, naturally beautiful vivacious girls; it was normal gravitating towards them in this hostile environment. If necessary, we would be their protecters, they would be our soothers.

Our first morning in Orlando, walked downtown for a cheap meal of toast and tea. Who do we meet, the two guys we met on Virginia Key in Miami. The guy from Binghamton, New York with the stringy blond hair and the little guy (Jockey) from Massachusetts. They were as happy to see us again as we were to see them. Encounters like this one became the norm for me, they always showed up in my younger years.

They were doing what Jerry and I were doing, drifting, looking for a chance to earn money, plant themselves, answer their question, what is life? We told them were we were staying; they came along, check the place out deciding to hang around in Orlando. Now there were four again. They suggested we take a cash job at the local Orange Juice factory, Donald Duck Orange Juice. Show up in the morning at the Temp agency, get hired on the spot, ride in a white Van to the factory. Some things never change. Jerry and I decided to do it, seemed simple enough, no experience required, sorting out the bad oranges off the conveyor belt at a rate of $1.60 an hour. That is all our time and effort was worth to them, it was oranges after all; it was 1973.

Yes, there were people from south of the border working there, like me and Jerry and our two drifter friends. Those people will always be there. Sorting out oranges is a boring mundane job; it got the best of us. Losing control, we started throwing bad oranges at each other. Things got a little zealous, we picked on our jockey friend more than we should have, regrettably, we hurt his feelings. At the boarding house the next morning when we woke, the little guy from Massachusetts was gone. We pissed him off, deciding to drift alone, leaving the blond-longhaired guy from Binghamton with us; seamlessly, he fit right in.

Don't recall what their connection was or if they met while wandering around Florida. Everyone has to have someone watch their back living day to day off the streets. We started out as four then became two, then four again, now we are three. Did not return to Donald Duck factory, don't know how we were paid, if at all.

We spent most of our time walking the streets casually looking for work, the next good time with whomever we met, all the while we met other interesting characters. Inspite of our condition, Jerry and I were enjoying ourselves, no rules. We hung out a Eaola park, a dangerous place filled with thieves, backstabbers and Narco agents while little old, retired ladies ate their sandwiches in the park, our backdrop. People standing around, spitting and picking their noses. Like a mine field, sorting out who was who and what did they want.

The undesirables liked to hang out at, "The Crazy Horse Saloon" right next to the railroad tracks, walking distance from the boarding house. Could not give anyone a cross-eyed look in that place without having unwanted trouble. One percent bikers hung out in there, trouble was accommodating if one wanted it. We learned to stay away from there. Eaola park kept on beckoning us to come around there some more. It was easy meeting people of like mind. They were all goodtime Charlies and yes, there were good time girlies. One such girl was a 22-year-old strawberry haired curvaceous girl from upstate New York, a little dingy minded, though responsible to her survival needs.

Like many people, she came to Florida looking for a future she could hold onto, finding work at the Orange Julius in downtown Orlando, walking distance from her low rent hotel room. Jerry and the guy from Binghamton attached themselves to her. She was naive though I don't think she cared if she was being taken advantage of as long as she was getting what she wanted, that was sex. She was a nymph! Too much traffic for me to indulge. I took the road less traveled. Not Jerry and Mr. Binghamton, they got on the bus.

We met other people, transients that managed to acquire a place to reside while they pursued their idea of happiness. It was always about the happy time, never ending pursuit. The boarding house we hid out at was nonstop good times. Surprisingly, everyone got along, the guy that got busted the first time we stayed there was now back, out of jail, happy to be free. He did end up with an incident were he pulled a knife on someone while we congregated, a bad guy. Calmed down when I reminded him, he just got out of jail; he didn't want to end up back in the slammer again. Mr. Illinois was busted trying to buy pot from an undercover Cop at Eaola park. I did not go along, instincts enhanced by my guardian Angel and the lovely girls from Ohio, keeping me and the others safe at the Boarding house.

Someone showed up with a full bottle of Librium capsules, good for alcohol withdrawal and anxiety it says. He touted them as a great high, I made the mistake of taking seven of them, an uncharacteristic thing for me to do, always dabbing first to see what it is, a novice. Being a pharmaceutical, lulling me in, after that, I don't really remember much about the next three days. Most of that time I was sleeping it off anywhere I could lay my head down including at Eaola park under the umbrella bushes that embellished themselves all over the park.

Third day I was starting to come around, lying on the grass in Eaola park, disappointed that my mates abandoned me. They were nowhere to be seen while I was in la la land. My guardian Angels working overtime to protect me. I don't know what I've done and I'm feeling so ashamed. Managing to get up off the grass onto a park bench; more aware and coherent, processing what happened to me, becoming angry over being abandoned. I noticed a white-haired lady walking towards me with a comforting smile on her face, in her hand, a cloth napkin. Now standing in front of me, stretching her hand out, offering me what was in the napkin.

What was left of her breakfast, she saved for someone like me. Said, "please take it, I try to help people in need of food, here in the park." Handing it to me, I thanked her, she walked away. Soon as I started to eating the food, realizing how famished I was; not having anything to eat in three days. She gave me tasty pancakes, and pieces of fruit. I thanked God for the good graces I received from this loving soul. Surviving my magical mystery tour.

In 1995 while in San Francisco on a telecommunications job, walking around Haight Asbury district after noon time, came across a young hippie, made the pilgrimage to the Haight Asbury district; his dream come true. Next to a store, passed out on the sidewalk, like discarded garbage; I approached him, he was coming back to life. Having just finished eating lunch at a Chinese restaurant, I handed him my leftovers, pot stickers and other good food I had left. Surprised by my offering, he thanked me as I handed the food to him. All I could think of was the elegant senior women in Orlando in 1973, handing me her leftovers saving me from starving. The circle complete. My deposit of love, to Gods universe.

My stomach shrunk; I was able to get all of the tender morsels into my belly. Energy returning, realizing where Jerry and the guy from Binghamton were. At the hotel where the strawberry blond lived downtown. Walked over there, establish why they left me to twist in the wind. Bad things could have come my way. They should have looked out for me. Entered the low rent hotel room, Jerry was in bed, Mr. Binghamton next to the round table, the girl who lived there at the Orange Julius, a block away. I would go there to confront them.

I asked my wayward friends why they abandoned me; Jerry had a who cares attitude, that made me mad. I excoriated Jerry for not caring about what happened to me. Jerry jumped out of the bed, came at me with a wild swing, I sidestepped it, the glass top covering the table I sat against, fell to the floor breaking in half. My wrestling skills instinctively came out as I gripped him, driving Jerry back against the nightstand; his head locked in my arm. I smashed it three times into the nightstand, immediately Jerry pleaded for mercy, I obliged, my anger was over. Uncharacteristic for me to hurt Jerry, I don't want to hurt anyone. I was built to love.

Wrestling is like handling a poisonous snake, can't make a mistake. Jerry wouldn't make that mistake again, not with me. There was nothing left to talk about, we put it behind us, back on the train again.

Eventually, property management for the boarding house became wise to us staying there without paying, locking the door to the empty room, our homestead. Now we were really out on the streets, though we made acquaintances with people around town, offering us temporary place to sleep. Late one night, no Jerry around, too late to go anywhere for a place to sleep. Deciding to go over to the boarding house on a hunch the window to the room we hid out in would be unlocked; open it, go in, take a rest. In the darkness, I walked along the hidden side of the house out of sight from the streetlights, walking towards the rooms window.

Found it open, looked in, who's in there sleeping, Jerry. He had the same idea, only an hour earlier. It was so good and comforting to see Jerry in there. I felt a sense of protection and well-being, like coming home. The next day, we decided if we did things stealthily, we might be able to sneak in every night till that room was rented.

Those still boarding there, new us, kept their mouths shut. We continued to meet new dwellers to the boarding house, they came, and they went. Two such people were a young couple, both eighteen years old. The girl, a little blond headed hippie, typical maturity for someone her age. The boyfriend was another matter. He obviously was madly in love with the little blond. Do anything to please her. This guy wore a black pirate hat, even had a fake sword he would play around with. It was hard to take anything he said seriously. His girlfriend had a clear mind, that was reassuring, they would not be a threat to themselves. That evening during our partying, I mentioned to anyone who cared, the Mardi Gras in New Orleans would be happening as we speak. I surely wished I could be there for it. The golden words.

I mentioned I had the car, but no money for the gas needed for the drive there. The young man with the pirates hat said, "I have money, I'll pay for the gas." His little girlfriend chimed in, "I want to go!" Just like that at midnight, the two of them, me, Jerry and the guy from Binghamton,

New York loaded up in the 1966 powder blue Dodge Coronet with the black top, got on the Florida turnpike north towards Gainesville, Florida, on the move.

Driving through the night, never considering, wait till morning to start out. Then the unexpected happened. A flat tire, I steered the car to the side of the turn pike finding as safe spot to change the tire on the shoulder of the road, barely safe in the darkness; as the semi's raced by us with a rush of cool breeze. It was scary in the dark fumbling with the spare tire removing the flat from the car, mindful of the jack holding the car up, concerned it might slide over, a safety issue. Adrift at sea, is that what it feels like? Before I left for Florida, I let my brother Sal use my car; in return he bought a cheap $11 dollar used tire with a wheel in Ligonier, just what was needed to be road worthy, in the trunk waiting to be used.

At first, having a tough time lining up the lug nut holes, muttering to myself, I cursed Sal, thinking he got the wrong wheel for my Dodge; all the while we were all tripping on LSD. The semis screaming past, a few feet away from me. The world was moving too fast. Stressed as I was, coping with the Acid, finally got the holes lined up. Screwed on the lug nuts, thanked God for protecting me; off we went, anticipating having breakfast at sunup in Gainesville. Perhaps even landing some local "Gainesville Greens" we in the pot community knew of it, a legendary smoke worth canvassing for.

Entering Gainesville, we came upon a roadside diner on the outskirts of town, a cloudy morning, a little sprinkle in the air, 8 AM, not much sunshine at that hour of the day. While in the diner, it was not hard to locate likeminded people. We happened to be sitting next to them at the counter trough, all having breakfast together, making conversation, an instant bond was formed (1973 so free).

Comfortable with the locals, asking them if they could help acquire some smoke, we were on our way to the Mardi Gras. They thought that was great, wishing they could go, though they could not. Saying they had pot with them (Gainesville Greens), when we leave will do the exchange in the parking lot. The transfer of money to smoke went smoothly on the road again, not a worry in the world. The Mardi Gras was a hell in a bucket list item for me.

When we arrived in New Orleans, apparent the party had already begun. Young and restless, we took to the streets, take it all in. I found a place near Jackson Square right next to the wall separating the city from the Mississippi river. The car would remain in this perfect spot till we decided to leave New Orleans at the end of Mardi Gras. Home base, a place to meet when we became separated; the car would be a place to sleep, our home, in the French Quarter.

The first night, I recall people openly buying drugs on the street, smoking pot at will with no consequences from the New Orleans police department. They had bigger concerns than marijuana in the streets. I bought some soapers, crushed them up on the steps of a building on Bourbon street, snorting them up with the help of beer. Revelers staggering everywhere; garbage piling up on the curb, bars and restaurants spilled garbage out on the curb for the late-night garbage trucks pickup and street cleaners. That happened at 4 AM.

First, the police on horses would come through, clearing the streets for garbage pickup, followed by the street cleaning trucks. Synchronized to expeditiously get it done, ready for the next days anticipated mayhem. Smiling, I stood back observing, my body leaning up against a building, the police threatening the stragglers who taunted them continuing down the street; cops lined up in a row managing clearing the streets. Big mistake for one fella, hanging onto a street light pole. His body hanging out over Bourbon street, laughing at a policeman warning him not to let go, stepping onto the street. The "Big Easy" transforming into the big hurt.

The taunting drunks grip slipped off the pole, onto the street he went, right in front of the waiting police officer he mocked. The cop grabbed his night stick with two hands, jamming, pushing this guy all over the place, bouncing him of the walls of the buildings, light poles just kept jamming him with that night stick into a garbage pile, with a loud moan, he dropped in. That was the last I saw of him, down for the count, only his shoes sticking out from the garbage pile, completely covered in food mush and cardboard boxes. How do you like me now?

Going solo, my nature; I had no idea where the others I traveled to New Orleans with where. Later, I would find them at my car, behind Jackson Square. I recall people saying they witnessed the band, "Rolling Stones" on a French Quarter hotel balcony throwing bead necklaces, onto the French Quarter streets teasing the people down below. Bob hope was the Master of Ceremonies for the year of 1973. As for me and my travels mates, we were completely consumed by the overwhelming event going on all around us. So, this is life!

At that point in time, the biggest party I had ever been too, for now, anything goes. It went on that way for days. The third day, I remember girls in the French Quarter, how they would walk up to a strangers, give them a big hug. I liked it, till this smelly hulk of a girl got hold of me, clamping down. Prying myself free from her Velcro grip, moving away from her, thinking I will never see that blimp again, going about my business getting high, moving about the French Quarter in a state of mystic and rapture.

Later on, feeling tired, deciding to go back to my car, get some rest and sanctuary. It was in the afternoon, people milling about behind the stores next to the wall and the Mississippi river. Deciding to rest my tired feet, approaching my car, having left the doors unlocked so the others with me could get in when they needed too.

Well, they were not the only ones needing a place to regroup. I opened the driver's side door looked into the car, what did I see, that huge nasty smelly hefty girl that hugged me, spread out on the back seat. The only thing missing was the paper wrapped chocolate covered cherries. I was not happy, I snapped at her, "get out of my car!" She got out, disappearing into the crowd.

None of my travel mates were around, I would be able to rest. Took off my heavy construction boots, settling back into the bucket seat, preparing my body for the evening. Before I could get comfortable, this guy comes along, sits on the hood of my car starts rolling a joint. Sticking my head out the window, "get off my hood." He didn't like hearing that, getting aggressive with his language. Instinctively, I knew this could get out of hand. Reaching down to put my boots back on, just in case he decided to attack me. It's a man's world. I would be ready to defend myself.

This thug sees me reaching below the seat for my boots, asks me if I'm from New Jersey, which originally, I was, (born there) though growing up in Ligonier, Pennsylvania. Instinctively I said I was from N. J.; he turns to his buddies, "he's from New Jersey, look he's reaching for his gun." Stereo typing the situation. That was just what I needed; the thugs took off leaving me alone fearing I would shoot them with my boots. New Jersey had a reputation; I was glad to take hold of; if just for the moment.

Later on, the others in my troupe came, joining me. All of us in the car, it was apparent we stunk like a garbage dump. Badly in need of a shower. Later that night, out on the streets, meeting people, we found out Tulane University graciously allowed people access to the showers in the locker rooms at football stadium. Take the tram out there. It's free during Mardi Gras. Turns out they were also letting partiers pitch their tents on the football field for a temporary place to mellow out, camping during Mardi Gras, so free and easy in 73.

One of the mornings, to the campers surprise, the band "Cactus" started playing at sunup, getting things going for the campers as they wiped their blood shot eyes open. Imagine that, waking up to a concert. Good Morning New Orleans! We took the tram out to Tulane. There were people everywhere milling about going in every direction. We found our way into the stadium, following the crowd, swept away by a flood of people, till we stopped at the back of the line, entering the club house showers.

The girls and the guys were on a schedule, which group could enter the showers next, alternating between the men and women. Didn't have to wait long before someone in charge says, OK, it's the guys turn. With that, the men and women entered the showers; both already in there. Turns, what turns, it was a free for all. Humanity at its relaxed best. Knowing me knowing you.

The showers were large enough for a dozen or more people at one time, showering just like the football team does it. No modesty here. The water drain stopped up; water elevated beyond the lip meant to contain it; water spread out into the locker & dressing area. No one was paying attention to the other, getting that dusty dirt and stench off our bodies. Paramount, though it was hard not to see the women were in there with us; everyone was comfortable, mature about it. Naked, not afraid. We had to stand on the benches to dress; effectively allowing us to keep our threads dry. These are the days of unpredicted unforgettable experiences, that would be a big part of my life, including "Summer Jam 73."

The next day, hungry, no money though the guy with the Pirate hat did feed us when we were with him, which was very little. If not for meeting at my car, we wouldn't see him with his little blond at all. Taking to panhandling, it was acceptable, many people were doing it with success, a sign of the times. During the process, I met this tall lanky white guy with a huge afro spread out on top of his head, like he stuck his hand in an electrical outlet; jutting his hair into the air as if it exploded off his head. He was from Lyons, New York, a small place in the middle of nowhere in upstate New York.

His name, Jay Johnson, immediately I liked him, he was smiling, a happy guy, a few months older than me. He would be celebrating his 21st birthday March 6th, last day of Mardi Gras. He joined our small group. Jay arrived in New Orleans via Greyhound bus from his sister's home in Orlando, Florida.

He was visiting her family when he decided Mardi Gras would be a good way to go. Now he knows us, and we know him. He had money, watching me move about meeting people; pan handling, a fun way to meet people in 1973, part of the young culture of the time, like hitchhiking. I approached this clean-cut looking guy, put my hand out, "spare change" the same time he put his out for me.

We laughed about it, his name was John Williams, from Penn Hills, Pennsylvania (Pittsburgh). We started talking, getting to know each other when John's sister (Buffy) joins us. For me, it was infatuation, instant love for Buffy, perhaps a little lust too. It was the strongest drug I felt while at the Mardi Gras. The power of Love. Instantly smitten with Buffy, she was a force of nature. Buffy had a brilliant mind, physically alluring. All of a sudden, I was on a different life path. John and his sister Buffy were at the Mardi Gras from Babson Park, Florida, where their father and stepmother lived. It was destiny we met.

John and Buffy's father (John senior) retired at age 40 from the United States Air Force, starting a new family and life in central Florida. Visiting them from Pittsburgh, John and Buffy decided to go to the Mardi Gras. Needing a ride back to central Florida, I gladly offered to take them. Blow me down, shiver me timbers, I made my choice. No turning back now, love in vain.

Together we walked back to my car where we met a distressed little blond girl with her pirate boyfriend. Turns out, she severely cut her foot on a broken bottle, (walking without shoes) now she desperately wanted to get back to Florida as soon as possible. That is when good guy Jay offered, his bus ticket, the pirate could buy one, leaving us in New Orleans for the remainder of the Mardi Gras. The car would be crammed with six of us. I was happy, taking Buffy back to Florida, I wanted to be where she was, she was with me.

The last day of Mardi Gras, we hit the road at midnight when Mardi Gras officially ended, just like the way we started out from Orlando, at midnight. Driving through the night again. A nasty storm moving in from the Gulf of Mexico, it was smothering the car with a torrent of rain. Wind blowing the car off course, a stupid careless time to be driving over those low-lying bridges; just mere feet above the water. The waves were crashing over the wall, smacking the passenger side of the car; silence amongst us. There was no turning back, nowhere to hide from the treacherous storm, white knuckles. I had to keep moving, we were over the water for miles. It was touch and go there for a while on the bayou.

By the time we got off the causeway, I had driven through the most violent part of the storm, no longer over water. We would be fine from there on out. Continued to drive through the night till the sun came up, stop, drink a cup of coffee. The adrenaline in my body was for Buffy, she got me through the nighttime drive back to safety, passion. Made it to Orlando where we dropped Jerry and the guy from Binghamton, New York off at the boarding house.

Jay Johnson did not want to leave us. He went into his sister's house gathered clean cloths, more money, together with John and Buffy, we continued onto Lake Wales and Babson Park. It was an extended reach for the unknown, where will this end up?

Babson Park, Florida, The highest point above sea level in central Florida (215 feet). The Highlanders, meet the Mountie from Ligonier, Pa. Webber international school, there on the shores of Crooked Lake, 150 + rich girls attended till 1973 when nine young men were admitted; Joe McKeon one of them, make history at Webber college. He was one of the nine blokes that broke the glass ceiling! No skirt on me mate!

When we arrived at John and Buffy's parents' house in Babson Park, Jay and I were struck by the remote coziness of this little corner in central Florida. Babson Park is a giant mound of dirt, rising above Crooked lake, the William's home had a high point view. The stepmother was a tall as women, 5 foot nine, large friendly women, graciously inviting. She had two young children, one not yet a year old, an extended family in progress.

Jay and I felt welcome, though we hadn't formulated how we would be able to keep ourselves in Babson Park or nearby Lake Wales. Jay did have his sister and brother in-laws house in Orlando. Friendly people, Jay and I got along as if we had always known each other. We were welcome to sleep on their couches for a few days, then go back to Jays sisters home in Orlando. Not where we wanted to be. Got to scratch that itch.

The first day we woke up in Babson Park, a sunny spring morning, served a wonderful breakfast and a crying baby. The youngest and newest in the house. After breakfast, we put music on the turntable, got stoned. The Williams family were Bi/liberal though they were people of authentic faith, that came first; common sense prevailed; no crazy talk. Family was everything to them and its conservative approach to life.

This is the pivotal moment I learned of the Grateful Dead. The live Skull & Roses album right there next to the stereo. Put it on the turn table, I loved it, the seed was planted, Bertha. Over time this seed would blossom, bloom into a wonderful attribute in my life, March of 1973, when and where it all began, Babson Park, Florida. Would not have to wait long to live it.

John Williams was a bit of a preppy guy with a hint of hippie to his makeup, a chameleon. He did like the finer things in life, would pan handle as well. Drove a Cadillac sedan, a used one, don't recall the year. It was a painstakingly washed, waxed and buffed shiny trinket on wheels. John left for a date with his local girlfriend, leaving the rest of us to drink beer, listen to music. John Williams, senior with wife and young children went to participate in the Babson Park Easter Passion Play. They were purposeful Christians.

When the Passion Play ended, the Williams family returned, Jay and I went out to my car, watch the stars, wait for John Jr. to come home from his date, engage him for a late night tokem, fade away into sleep. Buffy went to Bed, followed by the rest of the family.

While Jay and I were in the car, we noticed what appeared to be an unidentifiable aircraft, with different colored blinking lights floating above Crooked Lake, not going anywhere. A sensation came over us, suddenly, we felt pinned back in our bucket seats; couldn't move or fight it, mysteriously it was lights out for both of us. Something happened, what was it?

Next thing we are aware of, waking up with the sun, John came out tapping on the car window to talk with us. Wanting to know if we locked all the doors to the house before going out to the car? He said, "they're never locked." We said we did not. That is when he said everyone inside claimed they didn't lock the doors (those mysterious lights).

Consequently, John could not enter the house. Not wanting to wake anyone up, John went back to his girl-friend's residence, slept there for the night. Something unexplainable happened during the night; while Jay and I waited in the car for Johns return from his date. I have no memory of it, nor did Jay Johnson, those unexplainable lights in the sky? My first encounter of a strange kind, not having anything to do with a sasquatch.

A couple days later, we traveled to Tampa to see Leon

Russell at Tampa stadium, (Big Sombrero). John Williams approaches me, says there is a girl at Webber college, says she knows me, and she is from Ligonier, Pa. Her name is Jeanne Beatty, a student at Webber college, wants to go see Leon Russell with us. Jeanne Beatty and I had known each other since 1959 from Sunday school at the Presbyterian church in Ligonier, Pa. She came along, it was apparent she and Buffy did not get along, though it was Suttle. Both vying for my attention. I couldn't be bothered, having a blast at one of the best concerts I ever attended. Jeanne made Buffy turn her attention to me, something she had been keeping at arm's length, women.

Days later, Jay and I made our return to Orlando for a few days, needing his sisters address, have my tax return check mailed there from the IRS. Get that money, make things happen, live in Babson Park, Florida. When my check arrived, I got the help of two guys from the Bronx, New York. They were shady characters, though had scruples and a sense of honor; they liked me. They looked like and talked like the Marx brothers. They made me laugh, I reciprocated.

These two shiftless Goombah's were able to use my tax returns money, turn it into a pound of the most fabulous smoke they bought in Tampa. Jay and I took the pound of marijuana to Lake Wales where we instantly became two of the most popular guys in town. The pot was crushing it with everyone who smoked it. Everyone tasted, they got wasted, the Candyman yes, I am, with a little help from my friends.

Jay and I bagged it up, went about making a profit so we could afford a place to live in Babson Park. One of the guys we met through John Williams was Joe McKeon. Joe from New York state was the local source for smoke and other assorted goodies before we arrived. Joe tasted he got wasted, helping us sell the weed to the students at Weber college and local people from Lake Wales. Allowing us to have an instant group of so-called friends. Popular in the moment; it happens that way when you got the stuff, the Dude.

Joe was stuck in a lease, a two-bedroom apartment, part of a duplex at the water's edge of Crooked Lake, needing to get out of his contract. With the proceeds we made from the pot, Jay and I effortlessly took over the apartment, along with Buffy and an athletic local girl named Cheryl Love. Cheryl was an excellent water skier, worked in a show when called upon to do it. Her slender muscular toned body attracted Jay. Cheryl had that central Florida tongued accent, abusing the English language.

It was April fool's day; the fools were me and Jay. Jay fell for Cheryl; I was in the grip of Buffy love. How did all this happen so fast? It took a mere two weeks for this transition to take place. We did not know what the both of us were getting into, having these two vivacious beautiful girls moving in, live with us. Hormones erupting, spumoni swepted Jay and me away!

We had instant friends; our place was the most happening spot in Babson Park/Lake Wales, aside from hanging out with the affluent girls down the road at Weber College. Cheryl had her own car, a shiny 1969 muscle car (Cougar), her pride and joy, a help, my old car had no breaks left, metal on metal.

Now what to do about Buffy and Cheryl? Jay just met Cheryl, fell hard for her beautiful long blond hair, her athletic build, effectively they were strangers learning who each other was; there was a lot to learn. Me and Buffy teetered on angst, she kept me at arm's length. I didn't know

one way or another whether or not she had the same feelings for me, I had for her. Though she said she did; didn't
know how to go about it, love me. Hey, you've got to hide
your love away. We were all growing up.

Jay was on standby with Cheryl. It took a world of trouble to learn what's been going on around here. We were
consumed with what we thought was a new life, a future
in Central Florida, romance in the waiting is the hardest
part. Hawaii disappeared from my tortured thoughts of
love.

Besides, 20 years old, months away from turning 21,
Jay had just turned 21 March 6th at the Mardi Gras, we
were always in a good time state of mind, so many new
friends visiting us. The party never stopped, neither did the
music. We sold all the pot we wanted to part with, it was
skull crushing weed! Jay and I had the bedroom closest to
the front door, the girls had the bedroom overlooking
Crooked Lake. At first in my mind, it was just a matter of
time before the girls came around showing us positive feelings we could build on. That was wishful thinking, with a
little patience added to the mix. The Recipe!

After all, they were right there with us, not going anywhere. Life was moving real fast for us. When that young,
new things happen for the first time, an everyday thing, it
seemed. The days passed like weeks when it came to romance, that never seemed to be on the verge for us. Strange
days indeed, trying to sort out the emotions without losing
a grip on reality. How did all this happen so fast, was it
meant to be or were me and Jay chumps for thinking these
two girls had a place for us in their hearts? We were losing
control of our emotions, scattered like lost words.

In their defense, Buffy and Cheryl were both 19 years
old, they didn't know what the hell they got themselves

into; it had to happen, all part of growing up; evolving, learning the lessons of life. All four of us were in transition from adolescence into adulthood. Not an easy way to go, trial and error hoping no one gets hurt along the way, not a perfect world. The passion was mounting as if it was in a bottle, compression slowly building into our emotions. Buffy said I was a bright light; she didn't know how to be who I wanted her to be. I wanted to be loved.

Looking back, I would call this month, "Blue April 1973." The angst kept building to a crescendo, an eruption was coming. Hearts on fire, burning desire, my love for Buffy brought only misery. She didn't know how to unfold her love for me, limbo, paralyzed. Stilling learning the ways of life evolving into a women. We were all trying to find ourselves in the process of maturation.

Three weeks into our living arrangements, little to no affection being conveyed from the girls, Jay and me no longer holding back our feelings, we all started getting angry. Hissing and snarling at each other over sexual angst, without saying what we wanted to say; breaking each other's heart, only bringing pain. Pushing the envelope. Buffy could touch me, didn't know how to love me, devoid of physical affection. No shattered cookies here!

It was becoming painfully obvious; nothing was going to change. In fact, as it turned out, Cheryl was 100 lesbian, she beat me to Buffy, why she wanted to move in with us. In the moment we were living, this did not occur to me. Looking back on it, I was not wise to the ways of the world, deceptions, ulterior motives, DESIRE. Cheryl was not what she portended to be.

It was the girls secret they kept from us, materializing once Buffy and Cheryl moved in with Jay and me. No wonder Jay and I were losing our minds, we were playing it

straight, being honest about our intentions, the girls were having their way with each other in the privacy of their bedroom. OUCH! Fly in the ointment; Cheryl was jamming me.

Clueless about the truth of the matter, immature, we pressed the girls to show us any affection. Why are were going through this, under false pretentions. This should not stand. Jay now pressing Cheryl, she wouldn't admit her intentions were for Buffy, as for Buffy, I don't think she had any lesbian tendencies until Cheryl introduced them to her. A brilliant disguise! Buffy oozed sexuality, like catnip for men; perhaps women as well. I felt it the moment we met in New Orleans. Now she is bi-sexual? I'm damaged! Dang me, they ought to take a rope and hang me.

The realization things gone wrong, catching up with all of us; Jay became hyper angry with Cheryl; in a state of rage, he jumped into the air, foot plant his heel into the trunk of her shiny car. No one but me saw him do it. This would be the last time. When Cheryl saw the dent in her pride and joy, the shouting and the screaming got louder, more intense, twasn't me! It was then, I decided this had to end on my terms. I contacted the owner of our rental property, explained away a reason why we could no longer live there, easily settled, no harm done, it was 1973.

Informed the girls we had one week to vacate the duplex, the dust settled, our reckoning, we a had a week of peace and resolution; amazingly, it ended peacefully. We all grew up a little bit. Realized we really liked each other; why we moved in together. One-week later, Jay went back to Orlando with his sister and brother in-law. Cheryl moved home with her parents, the place she came from. Buffy did the same with her father and stepmother before going back to Pittsburgh for the summer. I fooled around and fell in love.

I didn't understand nor have the maturity or experience to guide me through this episode. There would be other Buffy's in my life my heart would ache over. I was crafted to love, an anchor on my heart. I would carry this heartache another year into the future, like a dagger piercing my soul dragging my heart around. When I love, it's with passion. When I lose it love, it crushes my heart.

I look around, and there's a heartache following me. The memory lingers on, I'm never really free. I disappear into my shell till I take a chance on love again or a loving women takes a chance on me.

I moved into Lake Wales with my friend, Bo Bo, a good-hearted guy, same as me, we bonded. Through Bo Bo, I met a guy from upstate New York, known as "Stoney." Young man who left New York to start a new life in Florida. Never mentioned family or friends he left behind. Something or someone along the way must have broken his heart, pulverized it. He never would say. Stoney was quiet, soft spoken; he did love to party, a real stoner. His life, suspended in place. Can't go forward, can't go back, building a mystery.

One afternoon, Bo Bo and Stoney with Mike Ruschak invited me to go with them to meet a guy, Jim Hess originally from Philadelphia, living at a winter home (504 Edgewood Drive) owned by his uncle "Leithy Chestnut." He was older than us, 28 years old, a hardened maturity about him. I had to meet him first to know and understand that about him. When we arrived at his house, Jim was gone, he went to the store to buy beer, leaving others who were there waiting to greet us as we entered his house. Everyone wanting to buy weed and other assorted drugs from Jim. Make us happy.

Sitting in the living room, drinking beer, passing around a joint, waiting on Jim's return, I had no idea what an influence Jim Hess would end up being to me. Door opens, in comes Jim Hess, five feet ten, burley guy diminished muscles he worked to build, exiting from his lifestyle, dark hair slicked back. Without hesitation or greetings, he sees all of us waiting on his return. Looks around the room, taking in the new faces, then says, "two chicks on the corner, anyone want to go check it out?"

Standing up, I respond, "I will!" "Come on" he says, not knowing who I was or my name. We were instant partners, built for the chase. I am a free spirit; Jim had lost his way in life; God attached me to him, him to me. We'll sort it out. Everything the rest of that day is blurry to my memory. Then, there was a girl named Donna Storey, a big girl about five foot eight, 250 pounds, round mound of love. Like Momma Cass, a lovable caring sort she was. Donna was one of Jim's drug customers, from a well to do family out of central Florida; out on her own, she worked a minimum paying job, liked to get high, be free from scrutiny.

She was kind to me; thought I was a sweet little guy. Confused as to why I was hanging around with Jim Hess. Jim liked to do his drugs in the privacy of Donna's house. Jim had secrets he kept from his family back in Philadelphia. Along the way, getting to know Jim, revealing he was an all-state football player in Pennsylvania in the early 1960's. Even got a scholarship to play college football till a knee injury ended his dream. Jim still had passion in him for football, though the life of a drug dealer/user completely removed him from that world.

I listened to the accomplishments he squandered in his adult life. Getting a grip on who he was, a good guy, a bad guy, or a confused guy. He was all three. Jim saw me as his little buddy, a guide to his conscience, even protector, buoyancy to his sinking life.

One weekend night shortly after meeting Jim, along with Stoney, the three of us went over to Donna Story's house to party. We liked to do a drug known as "Crystal Tea." Done responsibly, it would give me a heavenly sense of enjoyment much like clinical "MDMA", used for people with manic depression, PTSD and other mind issues, a miracle drug that really works; mind adjustment, helping me look within, learn to love again.

Like any drug legal or illegal drug, do too much, problems can arise. The crystal tea was similar to the small barrel shaped dirty white pills we took called THC tabs. I enjoyed the crystal tea (could smoke it, looked like brown sugar) and the dirty little white pills. Never had a bad time with either of them, memorable ones. Therapeutic for me, looking inside my soul, getting in touch; peaking beyond the physical side of life.

I was introduced to the world of drugs October 22, 1971, a Friday night in Edinboro when under the influence of alcohol, my neighbors across the hall finally succeeded getting me to smoke a joint after constantly approaching me to do so, after moving into Green Oaks. I loved it! Not an escape, a pathway of navigation. An herb, acting naturally.

My other neighbors on the other side of our building who also tried to influence me, learning about it from me, said, "If you like that, try this" handing me a pipe they were smoking around their kitchen table, loaded with hashish. This was one week to the day before the Friday, Duane Allman died in motorcycle accident in Macon, Georgia (October 29th, 1971). Why keep a mind and life stuck in one place, experiment responsibly, open the mind to new horizons; be cerebral, touch the universe, feel Gods presence. Time and space is a bitch, physicality the enforcer.

Enjoying ourselves, stereo blasting out tunes, our buzz cerebrally captivating, when Jim Hess starts acting unhinged. I wasn't paying any attention to his habits or drug intake, captivated by my thoughts from the introspective I was having. There really was an internal problem with Jim, he kept his secrets to himself, till now. Had he consumed too much of the crystal tea? Other stuff I am not aware of, making him depressed, then suicidal; so, it seemed. At first, it was a passing concern, as the evening went on, progressing into full out paranoia for Jim, the weight he carried was his secret, becoming our burden.

Jim talking crazy, saying his uncle Leithy Chestnut was a mobster, would kill Jim if he knew Jim had fallen into the drug wagon again. Like he once was threatened about it. This revelation was all new to me. Jim never revealed his Uncle was in the Philadelphia mob. Is it even real or is this drug induced paranoia? My happy time, beginning to lose its hold on me, this is not how a good time should evolve. Sadly though, it is a big part of the drug world, though people do not need drugs to go down that path; some don't. A chemical confusion of the mind. These kinds of experiences could mature a person how to handle, survive it. This was the learning curve. Now, my natural instinct to protect, kicked in.

Jim's condition peaking, he reached into his drug bag, pulled out a .38 revolver, put it to his head, leaving the rest of us in shock. He's going to kill himself. Though I was high, natural mechanisms brought me back down to earth (the power of the soul), I had to stop a tragedy in the making. I positioned myself on one knee in front of Jim. Face to face like a coach would with a football player on his team; down in the dumps, needing encouragement. I was not afraid of the gun, not for me, for Jim. I started recanting an imaginary football game Jim was playing in. Pure fantasy.

Making up a play-by-play account, invade his mind, keeping Jim from pulling the trigger. I kept at it till Jim stopped saying his uncle would come find and kill him, putting down the gun. I placed his mind on an imaginary grid iron, he was the star of the game. It worked! He put the gun away into the bag he retrieved it from, becoming happy again. Jim came out of it, even started to enjoy his buzz, he went from cheer down to cheer up.

Unfortunately, the next weekend, again at Donna Storey's house, it was an instant replay, as if we hadn't left that scene from the weekend before, stuck in a void. Once again, using the same tactic, getting inside Jim's head, calming him, ending the drama.

Between Jim Hess and Buffy Williams, my stress level for spring of 1973 was over its limits. My mind had stretch marks.

CHAPTER FOUR

Wanting to go back to Ligonier, Pa. Month of May beginning, needing a break, this adventure coming to an end, settle down, go back to a place I called home, Ligonier, Pennsylvania, no longer pursue moving to Hawaii. Put that dream to rest for now, collect myself, start all over with a new aspiration, travel through time into an uncertain future. Jim Hess wanted to spend time with his mother in Philadelphia, she was high up in Philadelphia politics. Someone of influence and power; locally. Together we would make the trip north stopping in Fairfax, Virginia, visit with Jim's friend, "Peggy Romaine." A musician, pianist, a good person. A reflection of who Jim Hess used to be.

The day before we were to leave, I don't recall how or where we met this cute sandy brown-haired girl with no shoes on, wearing Daisy Duke blue jean shorts; a tank top, nothing else, out of nowhere she descended upon us. I know, she traveled with Jim and me up Interstate-95 to Washington, D.C. area, where Fairfax is in Northern Virginia. It took a few days with her, realize something was wrong in her head. Too late, she's in the car, we are on our way north to the city of brotherly love, standing still on the run.

Among Jim Hess's addictions was alcohol. Traveling up the interstate, he asks me to stop at an exit, buy drinks and snacks. Turned out it was a bottle of cheap champagne. Jim sitting in the passenger seat, the girl dozing off in the back seat. Jim decides he's going to open the bottle of champagne. It has a cork, no corkscrew to get it out. Jim wants his alcohol; NOW! Pulls a pocketknife out of his pocket, goes to work on the cork.

Taking a quick glance to see how it was coming, keeping

65

my eyes on the road, when suddenly, in the blink of an eye the cork pops out of the bottle, into the windshield, coming back at Jim like a bullet, hitting Jim between the eyes, busting him open with a nasty looking sore, then punched off my chest ricocheting around the car. The cork eventually stopped bouncing about the car. I was stuck between stunned and laughing. Jim turned the rear-view mirror to his face, assessing the damage between his eyes, it made a mark. He had a bloodshot third eye. Wanting to better assess and clean his wound, he suggested we stop at the next exit with $8 a night rooms we saw posted on the roadside billboard, living on the cheap; it was 1973.

Wasn't much of a room, though it was clean, we were able to shower, take a nap, give up the room, keep on truckin till we made it to Fairfax, Virginia. Check into a low rent room there, Jim called his friend Peggy Romaine; let her know we arrived in town. Then we went over to Peggy's home, she lived with her parents and a few renters. O'Conner Macintyre one of them; lived in the below ground room or basement, fixed up like an apartment, a nice girl in the other makeshift bedroom. The center were all their friends congregated, made music, let the good times roll.

We didn't stay long; Peggy's musician friends were coming over to jam in the family living room were the 9-foot Steinway grand piano was in place. This was a free-wheeling family, pot smoking was part of the scene. Parents paid no attention to it. Not too keen on why it was important to Jim, for us to stop there. He was a far different person than Peggy's musician friends. Everything about this house and family appeared clean-cut, the cover of this book was different from the story.

The next day, we left for Philadelphia. When we arrived,

Jim said he needed to speak with his mother privately before introducing me, asking me and the goofy girl to wait in the car, a few blocks away. I dropped him off at his mother's Townhouse apartment, parked the car a shady neighborhood down the street. Standing next to the Dodge Cornett, wondering what the hell I got myself into, losing my patience. I didn't want to be in Philadelphia. I didn't have an exit strategy, didn't want to get swept over the falls, running against the wind.

The strange girl started talking crazy, I lost my tolerance with her, we argued, then she started walking away from me. I said, "where are you going?" She said, "get away from you!" I said, "you don't have shoes on, are you crazy? This neighborhood will swallow you up, come on back, please come back." "How in the world can you come from Florida to Philadelphia with no cloth's and no shoes on your feet?" She kept on walking down the street till she was no longer in sight. What the hell just happened? I was worried for her; it made my heart ache. This neighborhood did not look like a safe place to be wondering around in. It looked unforgiving. I prayed to God to protect her. My heart filled with lamentations for her well-being and protection. Can things get any crazier?

Jim Hess turns the corner, comes walking up to me, having givin his mother a heads up there would be guests this night at her home. Well, now only one guest. When I told him what happened with the goofy girl, he brushed it off like it meant nothing to him. She was his plaything, not mine. We spent a weird evening at his mother's house, me muzzled, Jim didn't want me to say anything that might upset his mother. If she asked me about Jim's third eye; I was to repeat what he said. It was an on-the-job construction accident in Lake Wales.

The next morning, we drove back to Fairfax, Virginia where I got to know Peggy Romaine better; a really good character who cared about what happened to me. Peggy measured me, what the hell was I doing, hanging out with Jim Hess? Couldn't process it. I didn't have my wings.

For a reason I do not remember, Jim instructed me to drive into Washington, D.C. The city was confusing with all the circle turn abouts. Driving around like a ship without a rudder. We ended up in a District of Columbia housing project. Like nothing I ever saw. My best to express it. We turned a corner onto a street that had more black humans on it than any city street I ever witnessed till Freak Nick in Atlanta, Georgia, 1994. The row houses had long descending steps leading to the city sidewalks, completely filled with bodies crushed together onto the sidewalk, continuing onto the avenue; "Shakedown Street."

The crush expanded from the row houses onto the city street from sidewalk to sidewalk as if the street did not exist. Quick passage was not physically possible in a car or by foot for that matter. We inched our way down this jammed street of people, like a cartoon. I look at Jim, Jim looks at me, what the hell have we done, we are the only white people in sight. Survival instincts took over. We moved along like a blob of molasses, I put up the peace sign. Jim says, "that won't help you here!"

Calling all Angels; nothing happened, making it to the other end of the street, turned, we moved on. Perhaps it did, never show the fear in your eyes. Only Freak Nik in Atlanta in the 1994 was anything like it. That was a city-wide party, what we experienced was everyday life in Washington D.C., circa 1973.

We ran out of cash, had nowhere to go, Jim checked himself into a hospital for rehab, his escape; abandoning me, left to my own devices, which was this car with no brakes. Peggy distressed Jim deserted me, effectively, stranding me. Really, it was best, no hard feelings, he was not good for me to associate with. He was a lost soul; I didn't see him as evil, or I never would have run around with him.

After spending a couple nights, a Peggy's house, I sold my car to Peggy's boyfriend for $50. Used some of the money for a one-way ticket to Pittsburgh international airport out of Dulles international airport in Washington, D.C.

Boarded a bus from Pittsburgh international to Greensburg, Pa. where I hitchhiked into Ligonier, Pa. a former Oppidan of this exquisite colonial town. Spent a week there, doing what I cannot remember, nothing I was after materialized. Then hitchhiked north to Edinboro, moving onto the summer of 1973, about to embrace my world. I could not have picked a more fun place to be than Edinboro, Pennsylvania in the summer of 1973. It would be a time in my life that would never be duplicated. This story until now has been a prelude, setting the table for "Summer Jam 1973."

CHAPTER FIVE

Memorial Day weekend, packed up my travel bags, walked to the west side of Ligonier out onto Route 30 (Old Lincoln Highway) put thumb up towards Pittsburgh, as I had so many times before on my way north to Edinboro. North to the land of fun and games, coeds too. There was no way my young mind could have envisioned what would transpire after my arrival.

Normally a 3-hour drive from Ligonier to Edinboro, hitchhiking made it undeterminable. About to turn 21 years old, not a worry in the world. Taking chances is and has always been a part of my nature. What me worry? Surviving the mistakes; navigating adversity. When I arrived in Edinboro, I went to see friends, (Edinboro students) at their rental house on Highway 99 north also known as Erie street. Just a stone's throw away from the Crossroads Diner. It was just before the beginning of summer classes, all the friends I knew at this house were home on summer break for another week till they returned for summer classes with the exception of two of them.

There was a spare bed I could sleep in for a week, then I would have to seek another location; set myself up for the summer. I had a plan. I would go to the administration building of Edinboro University, seek any available employment they could offer, filling their needs for another laborer in a diminished pool of summer prospects. Life was easy to navigate in 1973. The plan was on the mark. They hired me helping a campus custodian fix broken items in the dormitory rooms on campus. He didn't need my help at all, just told me to make myself comfortable, wonder off out of site, even take a nap on a bed.

I would be paid $1.60 an hour for 40 hours a week. Enough money to survive on. The cost of living in a small-town College in 1973 was dusty cheap. Job in hand, I had to seek out another place to rest my head, change my cloths, shower etc. I was a Rolling Stone, where I laid my hat was my home. Not just a song. It was ebb and flow, a window in time I was meant to go through. My yellow brick road.

Along the way, going to parties, I crossed paths with someone I had not seen in a while, even before I left for Florida; he was out of sight out of mind, though I liked this guy. Too many people to keep up with, running in all circles in Edinboro, ubiquitous. His name was Jeff Sayer from Buffalo, New York. We were cellar dwellers two years before, both entering school at Edinboro late August 1971.

We did not get along at first, he didn't understand me, my energetic excitable nature rubbed him the wrong way. He learned I was high strung, emotional, determined, he adjusted to it. Born that way, my biggest fight in life; with myself. Every soul has to look in the mirror. Man/women up against themselves, or life's circumstances will beat them down. The power and authority of time and space.

Jeff, a young man of high moral standards; could be judgmental. Being misunderstood was something I have dealt with all my life. I don't expect I will ever overcome this affliction unless I become comatose. Then people will complain I'm not paying attention to them. I can't buy everyone a pony.

Jeff was happy to see me, a little older and wiser, he was a settled guy, the kind that wanted to be married more than anything else. He was living with his girlfriend Lori in the (Coveview) grey apartments below street level on 6N east. Next to a place that did not exist at the time called Fat Willies wings, right across from Pac & Sac quick stop next to the hoagie and pizza restaurant businesses; neither no longer existing from better days gone by.

Our conversation made its way to "Where are you staying, are you working or in school?" When I told Jeff I secured income though I had two days left to find a place to live, he offered the spare bedroom in their Coveview apartment, said the landlord had yet to fill the two beds in other bedroom.

I was welcome to hang there till the room was rented. I accepted his kind and generous offer.

That's how it was done in the summer of this college town. Only 25% of the students would return for summer classes leaving a glut of empty apartments all over Edinboro including dormitory rooms. Very much like a Youth Hostel or a Backpacker, one did not know who they would be sharing an apartment with. Didn't matter, young and numb, a sanctuary to explore from. They would charge the renter for the bed. Fill the apartment, cut their built-in losses on the bottom line. Relaxed atmosphere, summer in Edinboro. No other place I would rather be in 1973.

I accepted Jeff's offer knowing at any time I would have to leave there; consequently, I would remain in the lurch for a place to rest my head. Most of the time I was a ramblin man. My first night in the spare bedroom, window open, cool wet mist of the northwest Pennsylvania summer night seeping in. Lying there on my back, looking up at the sky; not knowing where life was taking me. I focused my attention on the soothing music from a location I could not identify. Floating throughout the neighborhood air like a carpet of thick smoke, the music of Pink Floyd, "Dark Side of the Moon." The tone for the summer was set.

Like 1967 was for the west coast aka San Francisco, their summer of love, on the east coast it was the year and summer of 1973, after that came the disco era scene. A blimp in history. Life is just an amusement park. It was in that moment; I knew I was in the sphere of the spirit of the universe. Exactly where I was supposed to be in this world. Not a second behind in my timing, perfection. A happening was about to take place, I would enjoy being in the middle of it. The mysterious ways of the universe synchronized perfectly, nothing but a big ole jelly roll. Time is too short to wait, let's get it on!

The way people take the time of day to go to their jobs, employment, work, school, chosen profession, there were those of us in Edinboro who applied the same measures for our days. Those people will always exist. In Edinboro 1973 circa, were professional good time people. A temporary sense of purpose!

Most of us in our early twenties still evolving, sorting out life, putting responsibility on hold, taking advantage of our youth. Our older minders in their mid to late 20's put accomplishment aside, you know, a successful career, family or undecided. That was on their horizon. Nothing's changed, we had our approach in that era. The future was far away. Long before mobile phones, satellite television, personal computers and selective outrage.

CHAPTER SIX

SUMMER JAM 73

The thought of being in the right place and time gave me an understanding of where I wasn't. No real plans for my future, this had to be sorted out. Life lived for better or worse, mistakes part of the process. When there is no certain path, I would let life come to me. I didn't mind, I was in my comfort zone, no stress or long-term anticipations, nor disappointments about not moving in a pointed direction, having fun. A simple life, an uncluttered life. Forevers no time at all. Destiny moves at its own inertia, be patient. No expectations, no disappointments.

One of the first things I did, acquire a Postal Box # from the Edinboro U. S. Post Office, my address, P.O. Box 265, zip code 16412. My office and base of operations if you will. I wanted to have an address for my great friend and mentor, Joey David of Baden, Pennsylvania. A former merchant marine/seaman who gave it up because of Polycystic Kidney disease acquired at birth; an uncurable menacing disease he had to cope with and manage. A death sentence! I did my best to help him carry that weight.

Joey was an accomplished piano player and song writer/singer; one of those people who never leave your mind. I relished the times we had together communicating, a never-ending dialogue of interesting subjects between us. Always had a way of opening up the universe with dialog, go where it led our minds, cerebrally soothing. Late in life, enlightening communication is what is left to massage our souls; keep the window to your soul open, let universal inspiration enter. Searching for truth, there you will find yourself.

Joey helped me grow up, be mature young man, the six

years divide in our ages made a big difference. Joey's high I.Q. made him noticeable in groups of people; Interested to know what he was thinking. I was beginning to develop my intellect with Joey's encouragement and influence. Joey was a man of the world, I wanted to see the world. Learn all I could about other countries, peoples customs, cultures outside of Western Pennsylvania; Joey had the stories. He was about to embark on another story (experience) in Argentina. I had to have an address for him to communicate with me.

Joey would be gone from Edinboro most summer at his parents' home in Baden, Pa. preparing for his South American trip, in the fall of 1973 when he would travel to Argentina on family business. I looked elsewhere for new friends to enjoy comradery with; the "Summer of 73." I would not be disappointed. Joey missed it all. How different it would have been had he been in the mix?

Joey David was half Maryland hillbilly and half Syrian. He was related to Don Knox (Andy of Mayberry), on his mother Alma's side of the family. Joey had two Syrian grandfathers, brothers who left Syria at the turn of the 20th century. One went to Pittsburgh, the other to Argentina. Both of these gentlemen where natural entrepreneurs. They exceled at real estate and property management, one in Pittsburgh, the other in Pergamino, Argentina.

In 1960 when both brothers were now in their late 70's, the older brother in Argentina "Willed" his assets and real estate property in Pergamino to the younger brother in Pittsburgh. The time came when the younger brother had to accept the wishes of his older brothers "Will" after his death, gain control of the property, which he passed onto his grandson, Joey David. Too old to get involved, now up to Joey to secure. Don't let the bastards steal it.

More than a decade transpired since the older brother died. The property languished. With the agreement and intention for Joey to travel to Argentina, meet with a 27 man-attorney law group in Pergamino, Argentina his grandfather dealt with before his death. Legally secure this valuable property; make it his own, make deals, take care of the back taxes. Perhaps move to and live in Argentina; sounds romantic, maybe dangerous. Joey showed me the letterhead he received from the Argentine Law group.

At this point in time in Argentina's history, it was a country on the verge of collapse. Argentina's economy was in serious doubt, monster inflation killing the economy. The kind of turmoil that are historical in context. This, during Juan Peron's second presidency, made worse by the 1973 Arab oil embargo and an outbreak of foot-and-mouth disease devastating Argentina's illustrious beef industry.

Political violence and labor unrest kept the country in turmoil. Not the best time to be traveling to Argentina; Joey didn't care, this was his James Bond moment. Joey relished the challenge going there, a man of the world, taking care of his family business. He would visit Edinboro from time to time, mostly stayed in Baden the summer of "73." Focused on the task at hand.

Now that I had a temporary place to reside, a money-making job, opportunity graciously provided by Edinboro State University. The journey to "Summer Jam 1973" at Watkins Glen Formula One racetrack in up-state New York; mysteriously in process. There was no way I could have predicted what was coming next. With the help of promoter Bill Graham, Sam Cutler and Jerry Garcia, the notion put in motion, it was time for an event like this one. Altamont was now 3 years in the rear-view mirror, let's do it again. Of Mice and Men, this time we will be prepared.

My first day on the job, in the early morning hours walking down Ontario street, a block of leisure walking to the edge of Edinboro's campus, a short distance to where I would report to work for the day. I would pass by a house with a name tag on it. A two-story gray box house, very old, with the name on a wooden plaque (Epigraph) cemented to the right side of the house "Char Lynn." At that time of the morning, all was peaceful and quiet. The freshness of the morning dew in the air, a beautiful sun lit day, youth, blending my life into a paradise. A frozen moment in time, one that won't leave my memory.

Days at work were uneventful, however on the way back to the apartment I temporarily resided; I had to walk past the gray house again, "Char Lynn." This time of the day, the residents of "Char Lynn" were now out and about in their front yard. Throwing a frisbee, laughter in the air, playing guitar, drinking beer, smoking weed exhibiting an aura of happiness, no worries. Taking it all in, I thought, these people got it together, I must make friends, join them. One of the residents was a girl named Karen Hufnagle from Irwin, Pennsylvania. I was familiar with Karen; she was in my speech class with Dr. Crane Johnson, the spring semester of 1972.

Karen (20) had a blithesome personality and presence about her, bubbly. Rosie red cheeks to go with it. A petite little blond girl with hair cut short. There was a very friendly voluptuous brown-haired girl, Charlotte Pagni (20), she was from Grove City, Pa., wanted to be an actress. Charlotte was the girlfriend of Bob Welch, an older guy like maybe 23, Bob had short well-manicured silky sandy red hair, fashioned himself much like Robert Redford. A young man of few words with a mature presence about him. Mya, she was a couple years older than me, from somewhere around Pittsburgh, she would be the house hen, always looking out for everyone, a paternal presence exuding love. Though I did not live there, you can throw me into the mix, one of them.

The guy out in front of the house every afternoon playing guitar, Mike Walsh from Schaumberg, Illinois, my age. A mellow guy without a care in the world. Five foot 8 with semi-long brown hair, medium build playing his acoustic guitar, always with a smile on his happy face. Mike knew he entered paradise. Then there was J.B. (Jimmy Bruce), five-foot ten wiry frame, shoulder length stringy blond hair with the ever present five o'clock shadow on his face, toothpick in his mouth. Age 27, from Beaver Valley, Pennsylvania: deceptively smart. Loony Tunes had a place for him, a caricature.

His friend, John Drago, five-foot seven short blond hair with an odd frame where his shoulders seemed too close to his hips (sponge Bob), not much bigger than I, though he did have 25lbs. on me. John also living at "Char Lynn," Karen Hufnagel's boyfriend, what a character he was. John once said to me about getting to the front of a long line. Just act like you are crazy, people will get out of the way; It works! No one wants to mess with a crazy person. Could be incorporated in other ways to get the desired results. A tool for fun, I keep in my back pocket.

At the time, I knew not where he hailed from, I liked him. John was a Viet Nam Vet, now a happy biker, Harley Davidson. His place in this story essential, without John's presence, this story may never been written. It wouldn't have happened the way it did or at all. "Char Lynn" was a meeting place, though a group of people lived there. All friends and like-minded comers were welcome to join the party, when it came to having fun, they took no days off. Every day was a holiday. The benefits of youth; we may never pass this way again.

I joined the party! If I could compare "Char Lynn" to any other place in time, it would be the Grateful Dead's house in Haight Asbury district of San Francisco in 1967. We in the east were 6 years behind San Francisco; as was most of the eastern part of America, though Macon, Georgia had the "Big House," now a museum. The home and gathering place of the Brothers & Sisters of The Allman Brothers Band. Very similar, though we did not have a house band, just a band of gregarious friends, some were musicians, some were merrymen and lots of friendly girls.

Not long after my entrance into the "Char Lynn" fold, I had to give up my residency at the apartment of Jeff and Lori. No worries, I had another place lined up on Erie street next to the Funeral Parlor with an odd guy, a professional student, around 27 years old, strange is the word to describe him, a social outcast. Could have been in the movies. I brought lively energy to his environment. We co-existed in that house, seldom saw each other. We had nothing but Edinboro in common. Got to be adaptable to the gracious.

He was all alone except for classes on campus and a few geeky friends. It was a free place to live, only the lonely. Must have been my charisma. I was happy to have it for the rest of the summer. Back then, a bit of a vagabond, something time would ultimately change with a little bit of maturity and direction. Eventually find my way into a dynamic future of incredible and gratifying accomplishments with international experiences. Wouldn't want to be anyone but the me (soul) God created. Comfortable in my own skin, sensing purpose of mission, we all have one.

Stopping by "Char Lynn" every day after work, it was unavoidable, the way home for me. I found what I was looking for! Mike Walsh and I were fast becoming really good friends, kindred spirits. Mike met J.B. in Gainesville, Florida over the winter where they were both living their own version of a vagabond life, drifters, midnight tokers. Mike dreaming of being a Rock star, J.B. making a living selling weed and other assorted drugs of the time to college students at the university of Florida, candy man.

Now he would spend the summer in Edinboro wheeling and dealing, when the summer ended, he would go back to Gainesville when it started to become cold in Pennsylvania. At the age of 27, it was his chosen profession, a way of life, truth or consequences.

There were other places in and around Edinboro with the same vibe going. It was intermingling we did in a small community as Edinboro University during summer school. The communal living had us all connected. Our lifestyle attracted a lanky blond haired Dutch guy (Hans) from the Netherlands overstaying his visitor's Visa, wanted to be an American. I referred to him as "Great Hans."

Another group living at the edge of town on farmland consisting of Donnie Morgan from New Castle, Pennsylvania, John Rice from Ellwood City, Pennsylvania, and two other good time students. They had a rambunctious partying place, down on the farm. There were other farmland communal communities. We floated to each other's place of fun. But "Char Lynn" was the center of that universe; a short walk for me. People from Pittsburgh coming in and out of town, joining the good times, then leave, come back again another weekend. It was hard to keep up with all of them. I always remembered the girls I liked. Some I never saw again. It was a time of promiscuity. Seemingly as though we were always all fogged up. The happiest summer of my life cascading down on me; I'm so free.

Donnie Morgan, a diminutive, good guy, always had friends come to Edinboro from New Castle, Pa. just to get in on the happy times. They varied in personalities. Some were tough guy bikers with soft personalities. Others, more aggressive. One of Donnie Morgens friends was a guy shorter than me; he too was a biker. Built like a fire hydrant, muscular, imposing looking, one earing, pirate look. I liked him, we were friendly.

He rode an exquisite shiny Black Norton motorcycle. One of the nice guy bikers, though he told stories that belied that. Some of his biker buddies and he would go to Rock concerts in Cleveland just to fight with the stage security guys because they were known for their Martial arts. The bikers took it as a challenge; just having fun. New Castle produced off center crazy guys. New castle, Pa. had a reputation!

The entire street of Ontario was loaded with hippie houses and apartments though they were mostly students living there going to summer classes. The street activities where always there, oddly quiet and peaceful about it with the exception of the music flowing throughout the neighborhood. I cannot ever recall things getting out of control. Probably because most people attended classes. Not quite the same at "Char Lynn." Not every student living there was taking summer classes, they would rather be in Edinboro for the summer than go home to the Pittsburgh area and beyond, let it lose.

When Leon Russell's "Leon Live album" was available for purchase, I bought one. I loved Leon Russell so much. I played the entire three album set one after the other on the turn table in "Char Lynns" living room: much to J.B.'s chagrin. He had never known anyone as focused as me. I loved Leon; besides I saw that tour 3 months prior (March

10, 1973) in Tampa stadium (The Big Sombrero). It was very much like a "Revival choir," two grand pianos, Reverend Patrick Henderson, there had to be more than 15 people on stage playing so hard, the stage bouncing, I could see the microphone stands shaking. People in the audience falling, rolling and tumbling down the bleacher steps, the action vibrating the sound pulsating. A really good time. A great time to enjoy being young.

After that record listening session, from then on at "Char Lynn," I was "Rock & Roll Ron." The only other time I witnessed a performance like Leons was 1994 in Atlanta during the midtown festivals they used to have in the 1990's. James Brown and his big orchestra, couldn't stand still; roll me away.

All roads lead to "Char Lynn," a revolving door of people day and night coming and going. Rolling Stone magazine when it was a true Rock music magazine, advertised a really big show taking place at the Grand Prix racetrack "Watkins Glen," known the world over for its formula One races. July 28, 1973, rain or shine. Opening act, Grateful Dead, followed by The Band, closing the show, the new version of The Allman Brothers Band with Chuck Leavell on Grand piano after Duane Allmans death in October of 1971. Tickets were general admission, 10 dollars a ticket for an anticipated 150,000 attendees. Sounded like "binge fun" to me. Going to this event was up for discussion. But how would we all do it?

About the same point in time, we learned of "Summer Jam 73," we all became aware of an outdoor musical event consisting of local bands, taking place in Ohio at a state park a little more than an hour's drive away from Edinboro, Pa. across the state line. We agreed this would be something we should all go do together. How, renting a 24-foot

U-Haul rental truck. A unique idea, there were at least 20 of us that wanted to do it, chip in and pay for the cost of the truck and fuel.

The only problem, no one had a credit card nor enough cash deposit to rent a U-Haul truck for 24 hours. With one exception, Jimmy Bruce aka J.B. He was always high on something though he was no fool. After we all approached him about it, the good time guy he was, J.B. reluctantly agreed to do it, though we all had to pay our share of the cost. It was agreed upon, in a matter of days come the weekend, we would load up in the rental truck.

Saturday morning, people came to "Char Lynn" from all directions, with childlike anticipation we gathered on the front lawn of "Char Lynn." Giddy, patiently waiting the arrival of the U-Haul rental truck, party favors in our pockets, a beer run was made; we were good to go, so we thought.

Around 2 PM in the afternoon, J.B. and the truck arrived in front of "Char Lynn." We were loading up into the back of the truck, here comes Donnie Morgan with his friend G.T. aka Gary Tanner, the son of Pittsburgh Pirates manager Chuck Tanner, hailing from New Castle, Pa. G.T. says he has some party favors should anyone care to partake. "Yeah, what kind of party favors?" This was my first knowledge Gary was a small-time drug dealer. Back then, everyone did a little bit of drug dealing, real small-time stuff between friends and acquaintances, just to keep a stash of their own.

No one was getting rich, though some made a living at it to get by. G.T. produced a bag of Rorer 714 Quaaludes, said he had 5000 of them. They were $2 apiece. About right for that era of $1.60 an hour minimum wage. There were 24 people riding in the back of the truck. Between us, 150 quaaludes were bought. Most people would be knocked silly by one of the Rorer 714 Quaaludes. Those who did them often were amazing, the amount they could swallow without killing themselves and keep on moving; must be a chemistry thing.

I was not a fan of this pharmaceutical drug. It would knock me out, though if I concentrated on staying awake, I could do it. Usually, would take the interest of a girl to keep me on the move. I had other party goods, abstaining from the Rorer 714 Quaaludes. In the time it took to drive to the event in Ohio, 150 quaaludes divided up amongst the group, the intensity of that kind of high was slowly taking grip, and the tide rushes in on the people in the back of the truck.

Things started moving in slow motion, stuck in a backwash in June. Pot smoke filling up the back box of the truck, everyone drinking beer and wine. The party well on its way before the back doors were opened at the concert, letting us out of the cage. It had the smell of insanity.

The people in the back of the U-Haul truck went through a transformation. When our driver parked the truck, opening the rolling door, exiting the truck; it was like "The Night of the Living Dead." The people already in attendance sitting in their fold up chairs, on their Pic Nic blankets, about to be entertained by more than the music musicians would be putting out. Our group slithering out of and off the back of the rental truck, People watched in disbelief as they kept on staggering towards the stage, crazy looks on their faces, eyes rolling around in their heads, slobbering. Staggering towards the lake where the music was homing them in. Is that all there is? Then let's keep dancing.

The stage was on a small island with a mote like body

of water between the musicians and the audience. It was on the park lake. On one side was a small bridge the musicians used to get their equipment and gear onto the island stage. Outside of knowing about the bridge, hidden by trees, the water was the only way to the island and it's small stage. The band playing on, watching the zombies coming for them with wild eyed looks on their faces. They kept on coming right into the lakes water.

The musicians eyes bulging out of their faces, not knowing what would happen next; they are going to drown. The situation looked desperate. Everyone on stage in a state of apprehension, caught off guard, something like this could happen there, a wholesome environment. Security was invisible, though the public attending were good natured about it. It was a sign of the times, 1973, the last momentous year before disco invaded commercial music and the future got hold of us. The final conclusion that started in the mid 1960's.

The public pulled our people out of the lake then do it again and again, bringing them to the back of our U-Haul truck, dropping them off. It became comical, the locals assumed everyone too high to manage themselves had to be with those crazies from Pennsylvania. They brought everyone slobbering on themselves, stumbling, over to our truck, complete strangers; they delivered them all to us; walking the dog.

One such guy, they dropped off at the back of the U-Haul truck, a tall skinny white guy with a giant blond afro, jutting off of his head. Cut his platform heels in half, replacing the portion with penny nails, his new heals. He was wasted, stumbling around, stepping on people with those heals; everyone yelling for him to get away. Others, "Who brough that son of bitch over here?" Someone asked, another, "do something about his ugly manners." Others, "get him out of here!" Someone threw an empty beer bottle, hitting him in the lips. He started cussing everyone and their mothers. Eventually he passed out face down in the grass. Someone still coherent gave him a Rorer 714 quaalude, perhaps two. That did it, the remedy, down for the count.

Watching the circus at the back of our truck, J.B. and one of the girls in our troop coming back from the high weeds, (ring of fire) where they got it on (buns up) in a mosquito infested grassy pit, they grinded into. He laid her down in the tall grass; she let him do his stuff. Both wobbling back to the truck nude, unaware that their bodies were completely bitten up by mosquitos, exploding with red lumps, eyeballs drooping, dragging ass. That's what Rorer 714 quaalude will do to you, no pain, no mind either; disco biscuits of the 1970's.

A powerful sedative that effected people differently. Some people came to life while others like me fell asleep. How people could do more than one or two without knocking themselves out amazed me. This event remains in my memory like a movie I went to see. Couldn't be real! Alices Restaurant got nothing on us.

Well, now the seed for "Summer Jam 73" was sewn. We gathered ourselves up for the short trip back across the state line into northwestern Pennsylvania; on this day, we made our mark. "Don't you come round here no more," the sentiment. I wish I could remember more of it.

Days later back in Edinboro, J.B., after the roll in the tall grass couldn't get rid of that girl. She became in love with him. He was a drifter, vagabond heart, couldn't be bothered. He would roll with the changes; she happened to be one of them.

Watkins Glen: A Half Million Profit?

BY TOM ZITO
The Washington Post

WASHINGTON — Last month's rock concert at Watkins Glen, N.Y., has apparently netted about $450,000, making it one of the more profitable one-day entertainment events ever staged.

In profits the event seems to be exceeded in the one-day category only by prizefighting bouts, football bowl games and the Indianapolis 500. And in terms of ticket receipts alone Watkins Glen surpassed some of those.

Although promoters of the gathering, which attracted approximately 600,000 persons, will neither confirm nor deny the net figure, they have acknowledged as "in the ball park" estimates of about $1 million in costs. They had announced a $1.5 million gross on 150,000 tickets sold at $10 each.

"If these fellows actually made about half a million, I doubt very seriously that anyone else has made that much on a nonprofit event," says Kennedy Center head Roger L. Stevens, one of the country's leading theatrical producers, with a keen awareness of box-office results.

Within Hypothesis

Rock mogul Bill Graham, former operator of the Fillmore East and West, says, "I'm only speaking within the hypothesis that there is such a profit, but if a promoter were to make half a million, then I'd say it was the biggest net of any such single-day event in the world since the Clay-Frazier fight — unless of course Gandhi's backers had a concession on the Ganges River."

While music events regularly prove more profitable than Watkins Glen, most of that money has come from television rights. Prizefight box-office receipts peaked at $2,-658,660 for the 1927 Tunney-Dempsey bout. Even as late as 1946 the Louis-Conn boxing match at Yankee Stadium grossed $1,925,564. But as televised bouts began in the early 1950s, gate receipts plummeted.

Consequently, Watkins Glen appears to be the biggest box-office draw since the advent of television. The event somehow attracted 600,000 members of a generation weaned on the television screen—the same audience that has helped make the record-ing industry a $2 billion annual business.

Last summer's one-day concert at the Pocono

(Pa.) International Raceway netted an estimated $200,000. June's 12-hour soul show at RFK Stadium here netted about $200,000. In contrast, the famed concert at Woodstock, N.Y., finished deep in the red.

According to sources familiar with rock promoting, the concert (excepting the acts) required about $500,000 in advance capital to pay the groups their standard 50% contract holder, physically prepare the site and contract for the stage and sound construction. Jim Koplik, one of the two youthful promoters of the event who, along with Shelly Finkel, has been producing concerts in Connecticut for several years, refuses to say where the money came from.

"All I can tell you is that we got the money from investors who have to remain private," says Koplik. "And my lawyers have told me not to say any more."

Ticketron Suggestion

Leo Canonico, vice president and general manager of Ticketron, the computerized, nationwide ticket outlet that handled tickets for the event, does confirm, however, that Ticketron suggested the Watkins Glen Festival.

"We thought the site would be an excellent place for a rock gathering," Canonico admits. "So we spoke with the management at the race course and then suggested the idea to several promoters. Jim and Shelly came through with the talent."

Canonico denies that Ticketron backed the concert. "What we were interested in was the opportunity to sell a large number of tickets," he says. "We stood to make 50 cents each on every ticket sold, and for 150,000 tickets that

means $75,000. But we did not share, in the profits from the festival."

Koplik acknowledges the following "ball park" figures: $400,000 to pay the three groups; $200,000 to Bill Graham for the stage and sound equipment; $150,000 to Watkins Glen

...race track owners for their 10% commission; $30,-000 for cleanup operations; $30,000 for helicopter rentals; $30,000 in advertising; $30,000 in medical and police expenses; $30,000 for physical improvements to the site, including the drilling of 10 wells, and $107,000 for the

rental of Port-O-Let toilets (for a total of $1,-074,000).

"We're still getting some police and medical bills," Koplik says. "I'm really not trying to kide our profits from you, but we just don't know for ourselves yet how much we made."

BILL GRAHAM
... $200,000 fee.

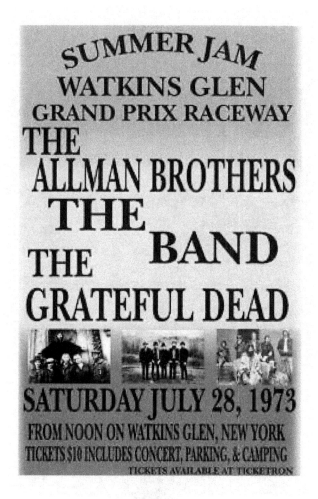

House in Edinboro, Pa. Ron Cosentino lived in during the summer of 1973

Char Lynn

Renovated "Char Lynn," where it all began. House to the right is where I saved Mary Krevaniak's life, Labor Day weekend 1973. Photo taken June 2, 2023.

Char Lynn before renovations 1992

Coverview Apartments

Coveview Apts. Window to the top far left is where I
heard "Pink Floyds" Dark side of the moon,
setting the stage for that summer of 73.

Ron Cosentino

Photo of the author taken from a 1974 ID card

Jay Johnson

Remembering Summer Jam '73

Joey David 1979

John Mark Donahue taken June 3, 2023, Meadville, Pa.

Driveway where the local crowd swelled as we were de-
tained and arrested on our way through Jamestown to
"Summer Jam 73." Back of truck was right there at the
driveway.

Edinboro Hotel Bar. Right across the street is where we
gathered Labor Day weekend tipping out beers to the Edinboro police as they passed us by with smiles.

Summer and rock festivals go hand in hand. These kids ... facilities, but at least the promoters put on a rock

Dickie Betts & Bobby Weir

CHAPTER SEVEN

July, the family dog growing, Mike Walsh and Joe Alexander a talented undiscovered guitarist living in Edinboro, jammed together in the living room of "Char Lynn." It very much felt like a community, with a family like connection between the lot us. Pretty girls joining in on the ambience of a family away from home. Hans from the Netherlands dancing in his knee length leather strapped boots; like Ian Anderson of Jethro Tull. He gained the prospect of an American wife; willing to marry him, keeping Hans in America. I would love to have bottled that summer of love, kept it for the future whenever life got tough, the struggle difficult to manage. I could open the bottle, go back to the summer of 1973, when we were all so free.

With the debacle in Ohio in the rearview mirror, a trial run now experienced, we wanted to do a group travel to "Summer Jam 73" at Watkins Glen racetrack in Upstate, New York. Mike Walsh and I got the idea, post a note on the wall, notice to anyone wanting to go to the concert at Watkins Glen; sign the paper on the wall, prepare to pay a share cost to go to the event. J.B. wasn't so keen on the idea; said he never was entirely repaid for the U-Haul truck he rented for the Ohio rant we went on. Wasn't going to do that again. We assured him the money would be collected up front, he wouldn't be in that position again. Deciding to start with $15 a person till we had enough people and their money to cover the rental truck. Mya, the mother hen of the house would be the treasurer. Go to Mya for deposit on the 24-foot U-Haul truck. Come one come all.

Ten days before we left for the concert, I turned 21, July 18, 1973. Joey David traveled to Edinboro; take me to his parents' home in Baden, Pa. Celebrate with him and his childhood friend Guy Pitch, once a small-time hoodlum in

Beave Valley, Pa. One of the few times I left Edinboro that summer. Never wanted to leave what was the center of my universe. Never been any reason, till now.

Many of us in Edinboro went across the New York state line, belly up at the bar. Kelly's right across the state line by a mere fifty feet, first stop, and of course Westfield, New York as well, just a few more miles up the road. Bands played in a loft overlooking the dance floor. The place was once a barn, now a frolicking palace to dance in. Long gone from its heyday. Lots a pretty girls and well-mannered people.

One visit to Westfield, Joey David and his cousin Joe Martinez had to carry me off the dance floor, my toes dragging in the snow, funny. They threw me into a snowbank reviving me. The girl I danced with helped me clean the floor off while everyone watched us wildly dance away, Joey, grinning ear to ear reveling through it. Joey said he had a special present for my 21st birthday. He said, "Guy Pitch will be joining us for the celebration." Guy Pitch was hung by his father from a tree with a rope when he was seven years old. When will I be loved. Having parents doesn't always mean you will be loved. They could be a child's biggest nightmare.

Guy survived, having a huge effect on him, he did bad things when he was 19 years old. Like rob gas stations and stores for little money, petty theft though it could be challenging. There was a time a Doberman Pincher attacked Guy in a gas station he was sticking up. The dog leaped for Guys throat. He caught the dogs jaws in midair in front of his face, yanked and broke the dogs jaw, dropping it to the floor. At six foot three, two hundred thirty-five muscular pounds, Guy was a big tough man. His father damaged him. I got along with and liked Guy. He formerly spent time in the Pa. state pen. Now he sold cars, a character addicted to sex, a misguided person trying to walk the line.

Waiting for Guy to arrive at Joey's parents' house, Joey informed me we would be going to Wheeling, West Virginia; about an hour drive south of Pittsburgh. We would be visiting whore house row in a scurrilous part of town in Wheeling, West Virginia. How it was allowed to be, surely the underworld must have paid off the local authorities. I loved new and off the rail experiences of all kinds, life unfolding in unanticipated ways; I embraced my "Present" from Joey. Never been to a whore house before now. Passed up on one from Johnstown, Rachels, over the mountain from my hometown Ligonier. The guys on leave from Viet Nam went over there, it's what they were used to while away at war, in Vietnam. Pay for play! They had the most amazing and humorous stories to tell from Nam I cannot print here.

Joey and Guy Pitch indulged often. In fact, one time Joey was kicked out of one of the whore houses for being drunk and unruly, the merchant seaman he was. He'd been to whore houses around the world; Wheeling, West Virginia was just another. After being tossed out on the street, Joey came upon red bricks, picked them up, started throwing them through the windows. The muscle at the whore house would threaten Joey to stop, Joey said, "Call the Cops!" Laughing and taunting them as he launched more bricks at their windows like Earnest T. Bass did on Andy of Mayberry. What cha gonna do, when the brick gets hold of you.

I have to say, the experience was very much the way it is depicted in movies though the class value of the place does make a difference. This place we visited could have been in the movie, "Walking Tall," the original from 1974.

Afterwards, we went to a local bar. Joey and Guy Pitch going on about their experience passing notes while I quietly drank my beer. The two middle-aged on the porky side, women working the bar, got into their conversation. Excited about these two young studs at their bar. Got themselves all worked up, thinking they may be next, Joey and Guy teasing them. Guy Pitch and Joey entertained the idea of doing these women, that made me queasy. "Are you guys for real, let's get outa here!"

Guy left the bar, went back to the same whore house, satisfy his insatiable appetite for sex. Joey and I waited; I'll have another beer. Back in Edinboro, we were closing in on the departure date; July 27 for "Summer Jam 73." The money collected, the desired amount, determined through inquiry of what would be needed to satisfy U-Haul rentals.

Everyone planning for this ebullient occasion, would make this the most monumental event of our young lives to date. Personal party favors were in hand or on order for delivery soon. I had mine. Back at Char Lynn, J.B. grew up in Ambridge with a guy named John Lewis. John aged 27, six foot four with that young Tom Selleck look, presently living in Honolulu managing a bar while going to college, coincidental of course. John visiting Pennsylvania arrived in Edinboro to see his childhood friend Jimmy Bruce, stay a week in Edinboro, then leave. While John Lewis was at "Char Lynn," I got to know him well sitting about, through our conversations getting high, he was a good guy; it was a pleasure to meet and know him.

He was so different from J.B. When you grow up knowing someone, you really always know them. The different paths we take in life doesn't change who we are, they enhance or degrade us, by the choices and decisions we make. The essence of us develops early, we see it in each other. Puberty arrives, all bets are off, the struggle heightened.

It was the night before our departure for Watkins Glen, New York. All was loud in the house, the chatter was ecstatically rapturous, anticipation was palpable; we didn't know it, come tomorrow, we would make history.

On this eve of happiness and excitement, I sat in "Char Lynn" living room with John Lewis and Mike Walsh, enjoying the conversation, Mike strumming his guitar. When I pulled out one of my (THC Tabs), took one, offering another to John Lewis. He had never done anything like it, though he was game to give it a try. This dirty little white barrel shaped pill was a combination of a mild hallucination and an opiate like high though I do not think there was any opium in them. Designer drug of the time I could handle. Cure what ails your mind, making all is well in the world, putting despair on hold.

John, days before, hearing about our imminent trip to Watkins Glen, stated he would not be making the trip with us to "Summer Jam 73." In the following days I worked him, trying to convince John he should go, a once in a lifetime event. Now it was the eve of the adventure, John just took one of my (THC) tabs. All he needed was a mental adjustment. As the drug took effect, John morphed into euphoria, it had that effect, why I liked it. I could stay in control, feel like I was in heaven. Really, heavenly feeling. Now that John was visiting heaven, once again I encouraged him to make the tip with us tomorrow. He said, "I'll do it, I'm gonna go!" John Lewis's presence was indelible to this story, a fulcrum part of it.

July 27, 1973, waking up to a beautiful sunny July morning in northwest Pennsylvania. Prepared myself for a big couple or three days, took a shower, took my time about myself knowing the truck for our journey to Watkins Glen, New York would not be leaving till early afternoon; right after lunch time for most people. Taking my time, walked over to the Dairy Supreme, just like a taste freeze ice cream walk up eatery. My standard order, two 35 cent sloppy Joe sandwiches, the best I ever ate, it's still that way 2023. A peanut butter milkshake also 35 cents, I was set for the trip, or so I thought. The Dairy Supreme was on the way to "Char Lynn."

Turning the corner from 6N onto Ontario street, at the other end where "Char Lynn" was located. I could see the mounting group of people throwing frisbees, milling about on the front lawn, spilling out onto the street. Humm, no U-Haul truck out front. J.B. said he would pick it up at 9 AM. Where's the truck, are we about to be disappointed? As I walked closer to everyone, they were all happy, there must not be a hang up with the truck. Where is it? The U-Haul rental business was five minutes away from "Char Lynn." What could J.B. and John Drago be doing, taking this long?

Entering the group in the front yard, I was greeted by Mike Walsh, wearing a clowness grin; "Ron, we did it, we're going to "Summer Jam 73," gonna get high, high, high." Mike, "where's the truck," I asked, "I don't know, they left here over 3 hours ago. Didn't say anything else about what they were going to do with the rental truck, we're waiting." I looked around, no one was panicking. I could see they went into the local forest bringing back long impressive tree limbs; would be used for a barn fire at the festival. There were half a dozen mattresses laid out in the front lawn, used for comfort in the back of the truck box. No windows, we would have to leave the back door cracked open for circulating air and light of day.

A car pulled up out front of "Char Lynn," Tim Marchase driving, three co-eds with him. Tim had the presence or looked like a six-foot four Ben Franklin, with a walrus mustache, a big man's build. He was a graduate student, older than most of us. Our lucky charm. Tim was articulate, he held a disc jockey position at the new FM radio station up the road in McKean, Pennsylvania.

They played Rock and Roll music. Tim; a really smart guy, generous and friendly. Glad to know he was coming along for the adventure. Well not exactly coming with us in the truck. Turns out the reason he and the girls were there in the car, set up a plan for the route we would take for the drive into up-state New York. The girls had exams that afternoon, they could not leave when the truck was leaving, they would be a couple hours behind us, taking the same route.

Map laid out on the hood of the car; they huddled around agreeing on how we would navigate it. Sketched out on the map, the intricate route that would lead through Jamestown, New York. Hanging a right towards the east onto Watkins Glen. Having no idea what would end up happening to the New York state Thru Way. No consideration! We were in the arms of the Angels.

I went into the house where I met John Lewis preparing himself to make this journey to a historical event, though at the time, could not have envisioned what was about to take place. He hadn't lost his enthusiasm for the trip, still feeling the effect of the THC tab I gave him the night before, as I handed him another one for the trip. I said, "You'll enjoy the ride with this in your head." Without hesitation he popped the medication into his mouth, off he was on his magic carpet ride. I was waiting for the truck to arrive before I swallowed one, deliberate by nature.

Walked outside to engage everyone in ecstasy. The chatter and the laughter was infectious. The U-Haul truck pulls up. What a relief. Like the pied piper showed up. Everyone ran to the truck, John Drago was driving, J.B. exited out of the passenger side, walked around to the back of the truck opening it. We were gob smacked, there was all kinds of food in the truck, like hundreds of dollars of food, drink, fruit, candy bars, a barrel of peanuts, loaves of bread, soda, and then some.

The deli meat, long sticks of bologna, ham, and other delectable meats. Cases of two-liter bottles of soda. Wow, we chipped in $15 dollars apiece, how did this happen. What everyone was asking as they moved the goodies over to the side of the truck, adding the firewood to the rear of the rental truck onto the overhanging ledge. Resting the wood there, then the comforting mattresses into the back box of the 24-foot U-Haul truck. Someone was thinking about an operational procedure, a plan.

It's a story in a story how this all happened. The night before at "Char Lynn" while I was convincing John Lewis to go to the big Jam at Watkins Glen., J.B. and John Drago where in the Edinboro Hotel Bar whooping it up. Bringing attention to themselves, as they reveled on about going to "Summer Jam 73," see The Grateful Dead, The Band and The Allman Brothers Band. As exceptional a lineup could be put together in 1973, for that matter in the history of modern music, universal magic; we found what we were looking for.

Sitting at the bar next to J.B. and John Drago where two drinkers not from Edinboro, just happened to be in town that night, deciding they would have a few at "The Edinboro Hotel Bar" before going back to Erie. Amused at what they were fast becoming a part of, they engaged J.B. and John Drago, two quintessential hippies.

Turns out they weren't the only two yahoos drinking up at the bar that night in Edinboro. The two men from Erie were crazy too. They wanted to know the details of how J.B. and John were gonna pull this off, aware of the event, the news feed about how big it was going to be.

"What you taking with you," was their first question. "Taking with us? Well, we are going to stop in New York; pick up a dozen cases of beer, beers cheaper in New York; we got weed and a few other party trips to go with. Also, 30 people including us, J.B. adds, "and my Doberman Pincher, Rebel."

Next question, "what you gonna eat?" "Humm, never thought of that," J.B., said. "We didn't think about being hungry or thirsty. We are going to be high through the whole deal, got beer." These two strangers all of a sudden became the best friends of all of us going to "Summer Jam 73."

This serendipitous encounter had to be divine. The two men from Erie where about to open a can of worms, hoping it wouldn't come back to slime them. Their unexpected generosity was just the beginning of our fortuitous adventure into the oracle. This part may be hard to believe, truth being stranger than fiction. We were living in our own movie. These two benevolent Robyn Hoods opened there souls to our embarkation into the history books. Thieves with honor providing us with an eucatastrophe.

Turns out, these two punters along with their mates back in Erie only days before had pulled off an overnight grocery store heist in Harbor Creek, Pa., an eastern suburb of Erie. Because they had no place to store their take, they moved everything, I mean everything including the cash registers to an undisturbed undisclosed place out into the dense forest. Using giant tarps to cover product with the idea it was only temporary till they came up with a solution, where they would move it all to. Then enjoy the spoils of their craftiness; they left to the whisper of the trees.

Giving directions to John Drago and J.B. where the "take" was hidden. Their only request was, we take only what we need, but don't take the very best. The night they drove the old grocery store down. That is exactly what John and J.B. did. The reason for the delay with the U-Haul truck. Now it was here; we loaded up the other necessities into the back of the truck. Meanwhile, John Drago got together with Tim Marchase, see how they mapped out the plan on the hood of his car. They fingered the route on the map we both would be taking to "Summer Jam 73." It was insane to think we would ever see each other again till we returned to Edinboro post festival time. One hundred fifty thousand tickets were sold for this event. That number was a miscalculation on a grand scale.

With thirty people and a dog making the trip, only three passengers purchased $10 tickets to the mega concert. There would be twenty-seven people and the dog, "Rebel" in the back box of the truck, with John Drago and two hipsters I did not know: sitting up front in the cab. They would be keeping John Drago our chauffer, company in the front of the truck. Our world in the back was a far different experience than they were having in the cab of the U-Haul truck listening to the radio. If only we knew what was going on up there. Nah, it's better that we didn't. We were in the back breaking all the rules on the road to Shambala.

Soon as the truck pulled out onto the street heading towards Jamestown, New York, the joints started passing around, people started popping pills, etc. We would take the highway, 6N to Pa. state road 957 cross the New York state line, stop at the first place we could buy cases of beer; load up and continue onto New York state road 380.

From there we would find our way onto Interstate 86 winding our way through the countryside onto N.Y. state road 226 into the countryside onto Watkins Glen International Racetrack. Easier said than done. Not to mention this being a long and winding road.

Tim Marchase with the co-eds following the same route two hours behind us. As the clock struck three PM, we were passing through Jamestown, the party in the back of the U-Haul in full swing. I was sitting at the very back end of the truck next to the sliding door, I kept open a foot high for air and light; John Lewis sitting right next to me, not a worry in the world.

We let the exhaust from the pot smoke circulate out of the back. Did we look like we were on fire, we were up in smoke. People were drinking down the suds, passing the joints, offering up something special they saved just for this occasion. You name it, that drug might be in the back of the truck. Jamestown is a small city spread out of many hills, much like San Francisco on a miniature scale. We could tell the landscape was up and down as we moved through Jamestown; like the circus passing through to the next city on the itinerary, the elephant on the street. The "Grateful Dead" would have been proud of us.

The view from the back of the truck was practically non-existent. What we were unaware of, the police cruiser tailing us. Oblivious, though John Drago doing the navigating had to be acutely aware we were now being followed; perhaps curiously so. His driving was nothing to be alarmed about, moving through the surface streets of Jamestown.

In the back of the U-Haul truck, we carried on like we were bullet proof. More fun than an amusement park, and the chicks were free.

Reaching the base of a hilly street, we started to ascend up the hill. We could here John Drago working the gears, like being on a Roller Coaster, the clanging of the gears shifting, about to climb the track up the slanted incline on our way thrusted into the history books and folk lore.

Beer cans piling up; start shifting on the floor of the truck; bodies blocking them until like a pin ball one happened to make it past everyone under the cracked open back door, out onto the street. Into the lap of the police; stalking us from behind, rolling and tumbling down the road under the police car. That was all the law needed; a reason to pull us over, roust us. At first, it was a non-concern, until we heard the police siren go off behind us.

Ut oh, I looked under the door, saw the police vehicle, lights on; I slammed the open back door shut. Announcing we were in big trouble, "It's the Police" Anarchy and bedlam, corybantic followed, the human condition at play. Shock and confusion interrupted our sunshine daydream fantasy. "What the hell's going on? It's the law, we've been pulled over!" "What are we gonna do now?" Arguing ensued, how we going to get out of this mess?" We gotta make it to the concert, the chant.

What magic can the universe produce now? The clock just hit midnight; we lost our mojo. Clueless; what was going to happen next, what about the guys up in front of the truck? What did they do to get us into this fix? Looking at John Lewis who had a big question mark on his face. His THC tab battling his emotions, talk about counter feelings converging on his mind. I'm happy, maybe I'm not happy, oh boy what the hell did I do to get myself into this predicament? All I could say was, "Sorry John, we'll figure this out." The conversation was wild, some people said the law could do nothing to us because the truck was a rental.

We had no obligation to its contents not knowing what everyone was carrying, that was not a bright statement. Some were saying, just get up when they open the door; walk out, they can't do anything to us. Meanwhile, for light, our lighters were flashing all over the place, fingers burning.

One guy in the back, recently released from a jail term in Virginia; for marijuana, said he was on probation, could not be arrested or back in jail he would go. Indignant, others said we haven't done anything to be arrested, let's all leave the truck, while others said, "no, let's co-operate, they might let us go, we can still make it to Watkins Glen." While all this commotion was going on, the police turned their attention to the three guys in the front of the truck, the cab. Oblivious, to what was in the back of the truck. Amazing they couldn't hear the chatter, sounding like chickens squawking.

What no one in the back knew, the two guys riding with John Drago up front were bagging up a pound of marijuana, sell at "Summer Jam 73." Not exactly a rolling cartel. The fiasco unfolds. When the police looked into the cab, what they saw, ounces of weed bagged up on the dash, in the pockets of these two entrepreneurs; sticking out for all to see, ounces were everywhere, busted. How did they know. Well, they didn't know. They got lucky; the universe has a sense of humor. Upon seeing all the smoke bagged up, these two officers became giddy, promotions dancing in their heads.

John Drago and these two soldiers of fortune where lined up against the street side of the truck. Hands in the air, they were shook down for anything else on them, palms up, leaning against the U-Haul truck. Meanwhile a crowd of locals from Jamestown started gathering at the sidewalk side of the truck. The two guys with pot on them were immediately cuffed: taken into the back of the police cruiser.

Leaving John Drago standing there, hands high, still palming the truck. The police excited about their bust, forgot about John Drago standing there, hands profiled high in the air. Crowd getting larger, vocal, "let 'em go! The crowd larger, ever growing like the blob. Hundreds all gravitating to this spot on the sidewalk next to the U-Haul truck. Giving us the thumbs up, "let them live to party another day."

People in the back pleading for quiet, paralyzed, so we could listen to what was happing outside the truck. It was important to hear what the police were saying, we had no way of knowing about the pot bust. Doing our best to remain invisible. Still believing nothing could be done about us; we would be on our way again. Now quiet, calm came over the back of the rental truck. We could hear the police standing nearby, waiting to open the back door. Curiosity as much as doing their job, they hesitated; savoring the moment; what would they find, pallets of Dancing Bears to be distributed at the concert.

Meanwhile, John Drago, the forgotten man, puts his hands down. No one looking at him, he walks around the front of the truck, evaporates into the ever-growing crowd of people mushrooming next to the truck, all yelling, "let them go!"

This is the hometown of Natalie Merchant (musician) who was nine years old at the time. Eventually, she had to know this happened. The local media was all over it. We were a happening of proportions not yet realized. We could hear people on the sidewalk asking the police why did they pulled us over? I could hear one of the cops say, "they looked suspicious!" Bloody 'ell, a U-Haul rental truck suspicious? People had to be thinking, these cops are delusional. What's so suspicious about them? OK, at this point I have to move forward in time to answer this question, mysterious for 13 years; why we were considered suspicious by the Jamestown city police. Why all of this happened in the first place, besides destiny, now a yarn.

In July 1986, while visiting my hometown, Ligonier, Pa. for my fifteen-year class reunion, I was sitting in the Ligonier Tavern bar refreshing myself with a cold beer, a state of contentment, when I noticed a burley guy at the bar talking with someone. I found this man familiar, though I could not place where I knew him from. Certain that in fact, I did know him from my past, where and when?

I intervened his conversation, mentioning he looked familiar to me. He said he was thinking the same thing about me. Together we concluded it was from our time in Edinboro. Pa., he went to school at the university as I did. He was a few years older, I remembered he was on the football team. He said yes, he was a collegiate football player. I asked, "what brings you to Ligonier?" He said his girlfriend was from Ligonier, he was visiting her from his home Pittsburgh.

I had to ask him, "do you remember the hippie truck that went to Watkins Glen for "Summer Jam 73," busted in Jamestown, New York. I didn't have to say another word, he had friends in that U-Haul truck, he was well versed on the details. One of those friends was John Drago. I said, "I didn't understand why the police said we were suspicious? Their reason for following us, ultimately pulling us over. His face swelled into a grand smile, saying, "John Drago is from Jamestown, N.Y., a local boy."

It took me thirteen years to answer that mysterious question, creating one of the best stories of my life. The year of 1973, a peace agreement was made with the communists effectively ending that miserable war in Vietnam. American society was set lose to be free. We really were in a brief moment in time and history were the country, at "Summer Jam 73" exuded it.

Soon as the police in the cruiser saw John, knowing his reputation as a local hoodlum from the 1960's in Jamestown, before he went to Vietnam; decided to see what he was up to, tailing us. The rest of the story documented. With John Drago safely tucked away in the crowd, analyzing the situation, he would be an asset on the outside of this drama trauma. The police forgot all about him, he was the reason they were following us in the first place. Well now that Andy and Barney are standing at the back of the truck. We could hear them talking as we calmed down hoping they would not open the back door, leave us alone. Praying it was only a traffic violation, let us move on; in the dark about the pot arrests taken place.

People in the back serving up their weed stash to the people around them, eat this, this too. Get rid of the evidence, I can't eat any more, pills were popping, psychedelics a dropping, as we sucked down copious amounts of beer, swallowing the dry weed. On a collision course with madness. I swallowed what I had with me. We would be off to the races now! Funny and scary at the same time, a kaleidoscope of emotions.

One cop says to the other, "well what do you think they got back here?" Funny, in their wildest dreams they could not have been prepared for what came next. Anxiety building to a pinnacle, are they really going to open the back of the truck? WHY? One cop reached for the door latch, we could hear the clank, yanking on it, the door in a state of suspension; in slow motion, rolls open to the top of the truck.

Whoosh, a cloud of pot smoke gushes out, smacks them in the face; they stagger backwards, empty beer cans rolling off the back of the truck onto the street between their feet; rolling down the hill. Three of our unit gets up, walks over people to the opening at the back of the truck. Jumping off onto the street, shouldering the stunned cops out of their way, disappearing into the huge crowd; street side, watching in disbelief. Who are these crazy people, why are they here and where did they come from?

One of the three exiting the truck was Hans from the Netherlands, could not get caught violating his visa, or back to Dutch land he goes. The officers processing what they just discovered, worked to gain their composure pointing for us to look to the back of their police cruiser. Announcing these two hippies where busted for possession of marijuana, they were loaded down. A quizzical look on their faces sitting there looking back at us; cuffed. Police, "We know you have more drugs and paraphernalia; we want it, and we want it now."

"Here's what where gonna do. We are going to shut the door, wait for all of you, put what you have at the back of the truck; everything's going to be alright, we'll let you go if you do this." Sounded bogus, we did not trust them. Besides, what wasn't already consumed was what we had left for our big day at "Summer Jam 73." No one offered up the rest of their stash; if there was any left to do so. Nothing was put forth at the back of the truck. We were gambling they were huffing and bluffing.

When the police opened the rolling back door, nothing

119

was there for them to confiscate, baron. When our hosts saw that, pissing them off with our defiance; now we were in for it. The authorities patience with us ended. One of the police officers grabs John Lewis by the arm yanking him out of the truck. No John Drago to drive, they chose John Lewis, who was out of his mind, a glorious high time.

John Lewis protesting, said he could not drive the truck, in his mind, he was concerned about the insurance of the truck, documents etc. He would have to be responsible for; should he wreck the truck on the way to the police station. John was speaking to deaf ears. An officer grabbed John by the elbow, pulled him out of the rental truck; walking him to the front of the truck, stuffed him into the cab, said, "follow us."

Police cars to the front of us, police cars to the rear of us, all the way to the underground parking lot of the police station and Court House. On the way into the underground building, John scraped the side of the rental truck against the door opening, creasing the box car side of the U-Haul truck. His biggest fear, a nightmare, woe is me, insurance papers! Calling all Angels; I'm not supposed to be here!

Meanwhile, one of the three guys that exited the truck, walking around Jamestown, wondering what he could do to help us. His name, Buster, from Erie, Pa. Found his way into a building overlooking the crowd, watched the proceeding from the roof top, safe and far enough away from the scene of the crime. The other two guys headed for the highway out of town hitchhiking back to Edinboro. They should have stuck around to see what became of us, truth or fiction?

Situated in the police station underground parking lot, they removed all of us from the truck, separating the girls from the guys, treating them like graceless ladies. We looked across the expanse of the parking lot at them; them at us in a state of perplex, far away eyes. What do we do now? The drugs starting to impose the group, hiding their drugs in their stomachs. Cheek and Chong got nothing on us.

First thing the police did, shake us all down for the drugs we had on us while other officers worked their way through the burlap sacks of candy bars, the barrel of peanuts and all the other assorted foods and goodies we had with us from the grocery store heist. If they only knew what they were sifting through. They would have arrested us for more than possession of drugs.

The only thing I had left in my pockets where antibiotics my girlfriend Louise Santella gave me the day before, for a sinus infection I acquired from her. I protested; the police took them anyway. Louise, a slender Italian beauty with long sparkling shiny black hair from Pittsburgh was not part of the "Char Lynn" scene. She lived in a girls dorm on campus, a studious student intent on graduating from college.

When I temporarily vacated the "Char Lynn" scene, it was Louise I slipped away to spend my romantic time with. She was a keeper, special in her way. I failed to look to the future. Along the way, somebody got lucky. Wasn't me. In retrospect, Louise was one I should not have let get away, she permeated love. A most beautiful soul, I let go of. Not meant to be part of my destiny. Glad to have enjoyed her affection, even if it was for only a short time in the summer of 1973. When I look back to the past for those who gave me happiness, I remember them as they were, a positive experience. Love returns to love; I will see those people again. When you love someone, you will always love them.

Don't recall the police finding much of anything left over

121

in the truck; they never said. Perhaps some of us had drugs on them, if so, the police confiscated them. We had no idea the entire state of New York was under siege from all the people converging on Watkins Glen and "Summer Jam 73," nestled in a place far out of the way of any large populace. Going up the country, baby do you wanna go?

The truck completely turned inside out, over under sideways down. All of our food donations were disorganized, scattered across the back of the truck. We had bigger concerns to contend with now; stuck in a void, where do we go from here? Into a jail cell, that's where! The jail was set up and divided into two sections. On one side of the jail house was an opening to a section of jail stalls separated by a wall, they put the girls in it. On the other side of the wall was another row of cells where the men were stationed. At this point, we did not know what was coming next, there was a cantillate amongst us; everyone chanting we were going to make it to "Summer Jam 73."

At the station, the police were nice guys, amused at our conduct, they arrested the traveling circus; just passing through town. Try as they might to engage us, we were too wiped out to communicate with. They stood there watching, hands in their pockets, with grins on their faces laughing as we made fools of ourselves. I jumped up against the bars of the cell door, reaching through them as if to grab an officer, yelling again and again, this jail will never hold me. I climbed the cell bars as high as I could go. They loved the theatrics; this doesn't happen every day at Jamestown city jail. Auditioning for the part of the town crazy. The guy that walks the sidewalks mumbling to himself. The local town fool no one wants to walk past on the sidewalk; unpredictable.

Meanwhile, Buster left the roof top of the building he

was scoping the situation from; made his way back down to street level. Walking along the same sidewalk we were arrested, wondering what he could do to help us get out of jail. Daunting as it may have been, he was digging deep into his psyche to come up with answers. Remarkedly, there was no quit in any of us. The universe ordained us to be at "Summer Jam 73," and by damn we were going to make it to the show; come heaven and earth.

Buster walking down the street, glances across the road to a gas station, before he looked away, a familiar car pulled up to the gas pumps. Self-service had yet to be introduced in the USA. He squinted to get a better look; the attendant blocked his view of the driver. The gas station attendant moved to the back of the car, pumping gas into it.

That's when Buster realized he knew who the driver is sitting behind the wheel. Excitedly, Buster runs across the street right up to the driver's side window, bent over to get a better view of the driver. It was Tim Marchase, the car following our route to Watkins Glen. Beyond amazing, it was divine intervention!

Buster, "Man I glad to see you guys!" Tim Marchase, "what the hell are you doing here?" Buster, "Everybody's in jail!" Back at the jail house, we were praying for salvation. Looks like our faith in prayer would be answered in the name of Tim Marchase; with an assist from an Angel named Buster. A guy who seemed to show up at our parties like a ghost, always on the periphery of our gatherings, then disappear. He moved about in a dimension of his own. Glad he decided to come along for "Summer Jam 73."

Back at the jail house, John Lewis singing the blues about the rental truck, with all the paperwork he was going to have to fill out. Getting higher and higher. The rest of us were beyond peaking, as we continued to entertain the police walking a tight rope between madness and reality. The jail cells were one door lets us into a corridor. To our right would be four holding areas or cells with their own door; bunks were made of a hard wood. We were packed in there like ten pounds of shit in a five-pound bag. All the THC tabs I swallowed were now imposing themselves, in charge of me now.

Becoming wobbly and loony at the same time. Incoherent gibberish talk going on. I knew what I was trying to say, couldn't spit it out. All the other guys were making the police smack the wall with laughter, crossing a threshold into an unknown place none of us had ever been before. Don't know what was going on with the girls on the other side of the wall. We could hear them, could not see them. Dueling anxieties.

Meanwhile, back at the courthouse, Tim Marchase getting the low down on what it would take to get all of us out of jail. Downstairs in the holding area, we had no idea this was taking place. It was looking hopeless though the mantra continued, we would be making it to "Summer Jam 73," no doubt about it, how could we know? We were the Borg, single mindedness of purpose.

Laying in my bunk, titanic struggle going on in my head with my mind; all of a sudden, the guys lying down next to my bunk sprang off their wooden bunks, joining the guys standing at the entrance of the cell area we were holding in. I sensed something sensational was taking place out view. Got on my feet, looked around the cell door corner. What did I see; big Tim Marchase standing there like Perry Mason come to deliver us unto freedom. Moses leading his people to the promised land, "Let my people go!"

Tim, in all his glory stood before us, he had to calm all

of us down; as we crushed up against the cell doors, like the front row of a Grateful Dead concert. Tim encouraging us to take a step back. Still digesting how it was he showed up before us. How did he know we were in jail in Jamestown, New York? The arch of the Angels. Tim's timing was impeccable. Miraculously there he was, Tim had answers to our troubling questions.

Cautioning us, we were not out of the woods yet. We crowded the entrance to our cell. Get a better look see, hear what Tim had to say, "relax, everything was going to be alright." He had the terms and conditions of our release set up by the court; conditions he believed we could meet. The rest was up to all of us to comply. Tim was the messenger, our shepherd, bringing forth the commandments of the Jamestown city court. Life is so strange, when you don't know where you're going.

Jamestown police arrested the Gang that couldn't look strait. We were a traveling band of gypsies, too slow to get the message. Here's how Big Tim explained our path to freedom. The law of the New York land was simple. With the influx of all the people converging on this tiny outpost in the upstate New York meadows. More people than can be held in jail and processed all across the state; the implementation of catch and release was deployed. Go before the judge at midnight (special session), we had two choices. Plead innocent, pay fifty dollars, come back for a future court date with no guarantee, abscond of the charges.

The other choice, plead guilty, pay twenty-five dollars, be released; then spend the rest of your life with a felony record attached to your name and social security number. As bad as that sounds, the impact it could have on one's life; in the time and context we were dealing with, we knew it to be a bargain, it was 1973. No one could have predicted what the future would hold, though we knew we could tell tale what we did on July 27/28th, 1973. Believing we were getting over on the law, winners and losers. Which one would we choose to be when we stood before the judge?

Tim says he needs all the money we had in our pockets; to get out of jail free. We turned our pockets inside out accommodating our release. Being there were 24 of us left; minus the three that escaped, the two that were arrested and John Drago, a forgotten man. The person responsible for us being pulled over and arrested at the beginning of this charade. With all admitting guilt, it would be 650 dollars to make the court happy. We would be free to go your own way. A far cry from the prospects we were contending with before Tim Marchase showed up at the jail house door. Tim had a halo glow about him, he was not alone. We reached into our pockets, pulled out what we had in cash till the $650 and then some needed, setting us free; was in Tim's sacred hand.

Then like a dream ending, poof, Tim was gone. Were we hallucinating? Now it was a waiting game till the clock struck midnight. In the time in between, we all dealt with the mind-altering substances we gestated. Most of us, if not all of us, would be feeling the effects of all the fun drugs we took for the remainder of the of time passing; before we arrived; the beast at the festival gates.

The girls went first, when it was time to be in the presence of the judge. When they were processed, it was the guys turn. Since there were more of us than the girls, it would take longer for the men to plead our cases. When it was time for my pod to enter the court, we were led to a large elevator taking us from the jail house below, upstairs to the court. The elevator had two sets of doors. One opened into the courthouse, the other into the lobby.

When we reached the courthouse level, the doors opening to the lobby opened first. Standing in the crowded elevator, perplexed at what we see, one of the guys says, "hey look, the lobby, let's go!" Still out of our minds, we had enough sense not to do it. Leave the court hanging, pissing them off, no one gets to be free. The guy who said let's go, left. He couldn't know what was coming, none of us could calculate it. He missed it all.

We saw him as a foolish heart; they would declare him not guilty, serve him papers making him return; with the prospect for him not looking too good. We remained behind, intent on getting through this wretched ordeal. The payoff worth it. Standing two by two before the judge. Elementary, just plead guilty, hear the gavel come down, judge acknowledge the plea, carefully walk back to the waiting elevator; return us to the jail chambers below.

I don't recall how it happened that way, but it was little me and tall John Lewis standing before the judge side by side partnering up with our pleas. The judge read the charges, asked how I plead. I, in my weak squeaky old man voice from the high I was maintaining to control, didn't want to piss the judge off.

I pleaded guilty in this crackling high-pitched voice, no energy to speak, I pushed the words out of my mouth. John Lewis's turn, "how do you plead?" "Innocent," John proclaims. The judge reminded John he would have to return to court if he wanted to keep that plea. In Johns mind, he knew he had to return to Honolulu, Hawaii; he had obligations waiting on him there. He could not stick around for an undetermined court date, commercial flight all the way back to New York. While John was arguing with the judge, before everyone could be released, I made my way back to the elevator exhaling as Johns voice trailed off in the background, back down to the corridor, leading to the processing room.

The worst behind me, having a better grip on my mental condition; though still feeling ultra-high, I began to relax, be myself. Noticing a newspaper on a desk near the hallway leading back to the jail cells, I picked it up. Reading the sports section. Once I read all I cared to know about, I heard voices around the corner, looked up from the newspaper, turned to my right, to my alarm, I saw people being fingerprinted, having their mug shots taken. Did not consider that being the consequences of pleading guilty.

Reality shook me like a 9.4 earthquake, catastrophic! I could hear our girls talking with someone around the corner from the desk I stood at. I could see through a window like glass into the hallway. A police officer, intently listening to our girls anguish. Still confused about what was happening to them, questioning everything happening to all of us. Why does it have to be this way?

Looking on, I could feel their sense of despair. I became emotional, the severity of what would follow us the rest of our lives had finally gotten to me. Serious business. I rolled up the newspaper in my hands, walked around the corner to join our girls talking with the police officer. An Angel tapped me on the shoulder guiding me to him. I was about to enter a divine moment.

Joining the conversation, picking my moment to speak, the officer turned his attention from the girls to me, wanting to hear what I had to say. Smacking the palm of my hand with the rolled-up newspaper in my hand; Saying, "This just beats it." The officer asked me, what it is that I mean. I pointed through the glass window in the wall, we could see the process room from the hallway we were standing in.

People positioned before the mug shot camera, others putting their fingers on the ink pad. I said, look at that, I don't even know what Jamestown looks like, now I have to have my fingers printed, take a mug shot." The officer, "you mean you haven't seen Jamestown?" Me, "no, I was in the back of the U-Haul truck, couldn't see a thing."

My distraught affected this kind and caring police officer. Without hesitation, he says, "come with me," I tagged along. Walks me to a doorway a mere ten feet from where we stood, opening it into the police station garage were the police shook us down. The door was unlocked the whole time, could have walked out of there. Says, "let's see if there's a cruiser with the keys in it?" I followed him to the police car waiting on us 30 feet away. He looks in, says, "we're in luck, the keys are in it, get in." "OK!?" Together we leave the underground parking lot out onto the now sunset streets of Jamestown, New York.

This kind Jamestown police officer treated me like an honored guest. Curious, he asked me what the benefit was taking mind-altering drugs. I said, "They open doors in your mind that are aways closed. Take you places you would never be able to go in your mind; enlighten you, a peak at the truth." He smiled, said, "I think I know what you mean, life can be mundane doing the circle dance."

Driving on the surface streets, viewing some of the neighborhoods up and down the hilly avenues. My host gunning the engine to show me it's power, said, "too bad you can't stick around, you could come home to my house for a late-night dinner, my wife and children won't mind." I wouldn't be writing this story if I had taken him up on his benevolent offer. I wish I could have, I respectfully declined. He understood, a good guy.

Returning to the police station and courthouse, we

parked right behind the U-Haul truck. The locals and the fire department in the back helping the girls, released before the men. Organize all the food and mattresses and wood in the back of the truck, preparing us for our departure from Jamestown, an improbable outcome. We were so free in 1973.

Parked under a dimly lit streetlight, taking all this surreal activity in, the police officer says to me, "get out." It took me a moment to seize what he was doing for me. This is really happening; God was with me. I would not have my fingerprints taken nor mug shot or having a federal offense attached to me, a criminal record. Why, because in 2008, I passed a secret security interview with a former FBI agent now working for Homeland security. For the purpose of working for a telecommunications government contractor in Baghdad, Iraq for the Department of defense. Part of my future destiny, an experience God mercifully saved for me.

The Post-Journal

JAMESTOWN, N.Y., SATURDAY, JULY 28, 1973   Page 5

Young People Were On Way To Rock Festival

47 Arrested In Area On Drug Counts

A total of 47 young people driving through Chautauqua County on their way to the Watkins Glen rock festival were arrested overnight by area police on drug charges.

The largest contingent, 28 Edinboro, Pa., State College students, was driving through Jamestown in a rented moving truck when police saw a contrivance dropped at 5:45 p.m. Friday at Fifth and Cherry

Crash Injures 5 Persons At French Creek

FRENCH CREEK — Five persons were injured in a two-car accident on Rte. 426 in the Town of French Creek at 8:23 p.m. Friday the Chautauqua County Sheriff's Dept. has reported.

All five were taken to Corry Memorial Hospital where the driver of one car and his wife were admitted. William Sawchyn, 57, RD 3, Corry, and Frances Sawchyn, 54, RD 3, Corry, Pa., were reported in satisfactory condition by the hospital today. Mr. Sawchyn suffered a cut lip and nose and bruised hip and chest while his wife suffered a cut temple and chest and shoulder pains.

A passenger in the Sawchyn car, Daryl White, 16, RD 1, Clymer, was treated for a head laceration and neck pains.

The driver of the second car,

Streets.

The group, ranging in age from 18 to 23, was arrested on charges of sixth degree possession of a dangerous drug and arraigned before Judge Lester W. Berglund during a special City Court session which lasted from 9:15 to 10:45 p.m.

Twelve persons pleaded guilty to the charge and were fined $25 each while nine others were granted conditional discharges after pleading guilty. Five of the defendants requested youthful offender status.

The driver of the truck, charged with sixth degree possession and resisting arrest, was not arraigned because of a police mix-up in processing all of the defendants. Judge Berglund set bail for him at $25 on each charge.

Charges were dismissed against one of the seven girls arrested because she was a foreign exchange student.

The students allegedly had a quantity of marijuana plus assorted pills but no exact information was available from police. The names of those arrested and all police records on the cases were locked in the courtroom this morning.

The young people, all from Edinboro or Union City, Pa., were riding in the back of the closed truck with a dog and a batch of sleeping bags.

Court Clerk Lois Sisk, who said that she has never been called in to assist with such a large special arraignment, described the group as, for the most part, orderly and polite. She said that at 11 p.m. the students, who had pooled their resources to pay the fines, were gathered around the truck trying to decide whether to turn back or continue on to the rock concert.

Chautauqua County Sheriff's officers, assisted by the Town of Ellicott police, arrested six young persons on charges of possession of dangerous drugs, sixth degree, and possession of a dangerous weapon.

The arrests were made at 1:28 a.m. today at the Falconer exchange of the Rte. 17 Expressway.

All six are in the Chautauqua County Jail today in lieu of bail or fines.

Four who pleaded guilty to the charges were: John David Kibler, 24, 1764 Hollenbeck St., Susaville, Calif.; Homer L. Partilman, 24, 4846 Fair Park, Dayton, Ohio; Tony Maxwell Simpson, 19, 5177 Embassy Place, Dayton, Ohio; and Stanley Knox Updike, 20, 1018 Clover St., Dayton, Ohio

Ellicott Town Justice Edward Jackson set fines at $100 or 29 days each.

Those pleading innocent before Justice Jackson were Clifford A. Davies, 1956 Grant St., Dayton, Ohio; and Davion B. Raney, 17, 319 Cowell Ave., Manteca, Calif. Bail was set at $200 each.

The youths were stopped by Ellicott Patrolman J. D. Dustin and Sheriff's Officer D. Jacques. According to reports they had a quantity of marijuana and a firearm in their possession.

Three groups of out-of-state residents were arrested on drug charges after midnight this morning by the Falconer State Police.

The first group, arrested and charged with sixth degree possession of a dangerous drug, were Douglas E. Richard, 23, of Nears, Mich.; Debi L. Tolbert, 18, of Marion, Ohio; Edward A. Neglio, 26, of New Haven, Conn.; Charles D. Fagan, 23, of Warren, Ohio, and Ronald S. Meade, 24, of Sharpesville, Pa. They posted $25 bail each and will appear before an Ellicott Town Justice Monday night.

The second group was arrested on a felony charge of third and sixth degree possession of a dangerous drug. Appearing before Ellery Town Justice Gordon Oste, this morning were Steven R. Sterling, 23, of Fort Wayne, Ind.; Michael R. Stuerzenberger, 21, of Fort Wayne, Ind.; and Mark Wood-

mansee, 21, of Bloomington, Ind.

Police reported they had arrested a third group which was still in the process of being charged.

Investigating policemen reported that several pounds of marijuana had been confiscated.

Arrests were made by Sgt. G. W. Knight and Trps. G. W. Rowe and R. F. Barush.

Arrested about 12:10 a.m. by Falconer Village Police on sixth degree charges of possession of a dangerous drug were: Ralph J. Bredon, 22, Berea, Ohio; Randall F. Glenn, 27, Berea, Ohio; and John D. Irvin, 21, Daynesville, Ohio. Irvin was also charged with possession of instruments to administer drugs.

The group was arraigned before Town of Ellicott Justice Edward Jackson, fined and released.

Falconer village policemen G. A. Beckeronk and R. A. Wilson made the arrests.

City Police arrested two Cuyahoga Falls, Ohio youths at 12:45 a.m. today on East Second Street.

John C. Heidel, 19, of 265 Elmwood Ave., posted $15 bail for a sixth degree possession of a dangerous drug and $10 on a speeding count. James L. Harris, 19 of the same city, posted $15 bail on a sixth degree drug charge.

Solid Waste Unit Criticized

BEMUS POINT — Ellery Supervisor Arden Johnson sharp

refuse taken to the Town of Stockton landfill site.

committee has gone unanswered. The whole thing seems

requiring all solid waste agreements between towns and the

CHAPTER SEVEN PART TWO

Standing at the back of our rental truck, mesmerized by what just happened, counting my blessings, looking in at all the activity going on inside the back box of our rental truck. Everyone earnestly in there, preparing for another joyous occasion. How respectful the fireman handled our goods, smiling and laughing with our girls. The locals couldn't have been more respectful; showered upon us with their abiding devotion. They must have sensed a momentous happening about to take place, sharing a small part of it, their workmen like efforts. See us safely on our way, that's what love will do for you.

My mind floating like an out of body experience, watching the kind police officer drive the cruiser into the underground parking lot of the police station and courthouse. We couldn't see them, could feel them, surrounded by Angels, protected. A mystic presence engulfed the moment like a lost ship in the fog seeing the lighthouse light, the safety of land, we were it. I will never forget the feeling, a paternal presence in the womb of Jamestown, New York. An improbable happening, finding its way to realization.

Snapping out of a divine moment, I could see the rest of our troop exiting the building walking up the inclined driveway out of the police station garage, a ragtag wary group they were. Happy days are here again. Looking around for the hidden movie cameras, this had to be a movie, the soundtrack waiting for us at Watkins Glen International speedway. Load em up, get em out.

The guys piled into the back of the U-Haul rental truck, John Drago back behind the wheel. What was he doing through all of this? Rounding up the locals, after all, he was one of them, juxtaposed in a quandary. Everyone safely back in the U-Haul truck; sitting in the same sitting spot, I was in when this made news on ABC, NBC and CBS evening telecast as the largest bust in Jamestown, New York; since prohibition in the 1930's. Fitting, we marked our place in Jamestown, New York local folklore and Edinboro, Pennsylvania. Who could forget this really happened July 27th, 1973. Can't get it out of my head.

Tim Marchase with the co-eds in the car leading the way out of town till we were safely on our way, John and the rental truck take the lead the rest of the way to Watkins Glen, once we made it to the outskirts of town. John geared up, the truck started moving, the mantra still ticking, we are going to make it to "Summer Jam 73," even though only three people had purchased tickets. A bold act on the part of the rest of us, we could not have mentally prepared ourselves for what would be waiting once we passed the great divide from thruway into disaster area. Unexpected obstacles remained in front of us. Onward into the unknown valley of the sublime; fearing no evil.

Determined guests of honor leaving behind a past we will never be able to recover. Time moves on, as does the culture. We reverently reflect. Tim Marchase and John guided the truck to the outskirts of Jamestown leaving the bright lights of the little city in our rearview mirror. Discreetly heading east towards Watkins Glen, down roads surrounded by the darkness of the forest, alone in the night, counting our blessings, what else could go wrong?

With that thought in mind, from behind the U-Haul truck came the sound of a police siren, through the crack left open in the back door, seeing the reflection of blue lights shinning into our truck. Bent over to take a look, saw a New York State policeman pulling us over. Oh no, not again! Hearing the door to the driver's side of the rental truck open and slam shut. It was John Drago responding to being pulled over. John walks back towards the Trooper walking towards him like they were about to draw.

Lights flashing, what is it now? Everyone in the back of the truck quiet wanting to listen in on what was being said. The only one talking was John Drago, in an agitated state of mind. John, "we just got out of Jamestown city jail, you can call them, we got nothing for you to find. Don't believe me, call them!" That is exactly what that New York state trooper did. Why go through unnecessary paperwork? We waited for his response. It came surprisingly fast. The trooper got off the radio motioning to John, waving his hand, we were free to ramble on.

Safely past the gauntlet, like a salmon making its way upstream past the paws of the Grizzley Bears, avoiding the same old blues again. John Drago's steady hands, his will to succeed held the road safely through the night; (really, an unsung hero), the rest of us continued dealing with our chosen state of high mindedness. Amazingly, no one overdosed; at least not to the point of needing medical attention. I was sure there were cameras, hidden somewhere, had to be we were in a movie, celluloid hero's. No one lives like this, except the Grateful Dead. We will collaborate at the meet.

Turns out, all across the state of New York, a plan was implemented at the state police level to do a catch and release, with the choice of $50 innocent and $25 guilty; what we experienced in Jamestown, N.Y. Standard procedure how to deal with a multitude of arrests across New York state; overwhelming the system like a synthetic virus. My friend from Meadville, Pa. John Mark Donahue, said this type of arrest happened to him on the way to Watkins Glen. He was in a 1950's Chevy type truck/van with his entourage when they got busted traveling to "Summer Jam 73."

Gimme your money please. The same thing! Better returns for the state of New York than the stock market. Rolling in the deep money. Catch us if you can!

Not long after the New York state trooper let us go, in the darkness of the container of the truck, I could see the light. Not the light from above, the one coming from a joint being lit up. How could this be, I thought? Everything we had was confiscated, where did this come from? The answer to that question was elementary; our friends in Jamestown provided the herb. Yes, we had plenty of time to plead our case to the locals about what the Law been doing to us. They responded kindly; we would not leave Jamestown empty handed. Roll another one, just like the other one.

The joints kept coming, the chatter started picking up amongst us, and it stoned me. What the hell just happened to all of us, thinking, asking one another? Are there more obstacles for us to hurdle on the way to the promised land? Having no idea what would be waiting for our big day out, once the U-Haul truck made its way into no man's land at the outskirts of Watkins Glen. We forged on; John Drago trusted to take the long way there. His steady hands at the wheel. He was the only one who was not effected by a mouthful of drugs. Running on empty. Only Rasputin could swallow that many drugs and survive.

Moving along in the dark on that highway in the sky, we crept closer to the back of the line, passing automobiles left behind, abandoned like a war zone. People could no longer make passage into the party zone, continuing on foot to outskirts of a disaster area. One way out, no way in, come one come all. Thirty miles out from the encampment known as a rock concert in the bush of New York state. We came to our first point of contact with the New York state police roadblock. Most of us were asleep, to weary to pay attention to the sounds of distant voices in the darkness of the early morning hours. Tim Marchase right behind us, his car following closely; not become separated.

We needed Tim and the girls following us. We had a story to tell the New York state police, why they were following us into the disaster area. First to speak with them was John Drago. As the state troopers told him, it's been declared a disaster area, turn around can't go any further into this jungle known as "Summer Jam 73." John said, "We have food and water for the people, the car behind us are the workers, they will distribute the feed to the people." That was music to the New York state troopers ears, mercifully waving us on. Arriving late to the event with this huge truck made them believe us, if they only knew what we been through. All we had were two fish and a loaf of bread. We embraced our sublunary moment. We can be hero's for just one day.

Since food and water were the biggest reason, the most urgent one, people needed to eat and hydrate, they waived John along; Tim dutifully followed, no other questions asked, not even a peek inside the truck. Brilliant, John and Tim still thinking coherently when we all left Jamestown city jail. They had the foresight to know what was happening at the other end of this journey, listening to the radio about the immovable object, the New York state Thruway. I don't recall all the roadblocks they navigated through, though it was all of them without a hitch. We were in! Let's see action; let's see people, let's see freedom, let's see who cares. Gonna get to where we're gonna end up.

John guided the truck far and deep into the concert area; we drove on the closest road to the stage. Passing it about 1000 yards away, seemingly close by virtue of the vastness' of it all. Navigated through, driving beyond the emergency area with tents for the overdoses, broken legs etc.; cyclone fenced off. A place were the helicopters could bring the musicians into the heart of the sea of people they would perform for. John found a place on the other side of the emergency area not far away from the stage, on the road we entered leading to it. Nothing is everything; if for nothing, solely by the music, we'll be free.

Parking the U-Haul truck on a slight incline. Leaving the backend of the truck; the rear end hunched into the air, a nice 4-foot gap underneath the truck providing umbriferous shade if we wanted it. This would come in handy as the sun emerged with a vengeance from the eastern horizon, like a blazing red rubber ball. I'm gonna hurt you! Few of us awake, some not wanting to wake up just yet, others like me wanting to get a jump on things or jump out of my skin; it was 5:30 AM, just a sliver of sunlight on the horizon hinting its arrival. The music would start at noon with the Grateful Dead. This would be my first experience enjoying the music and vibe of The Grateful Dead in concert. It would stick with me the rest of my life.

My soul would not have to been in the right time and place in this world without The Grateful Dead, The Allman Brothers Band and The Band all in the same place in time. It doesn't get any better than this; happy belated 21st birthday to me, alive and well in 1973, no other place I would want to be. A knock on the rolling door, I opened the back of the rental truck in the gloaming of the morning, standing there watching me, big Tim Marchase. He wanted to get his hands on one of the watermelons knowing it would hydrate us, we hadn't much drinkable water.

The coeds waiting, watching as I handed down the watermelon to Tim. He says, "why don't you come with us, we might get lucky, weave our way close as we can to the stage." All of this surreal, reaching the mountain top, "OK, I'm in! All the young dudes, people everywhere, never seen so many people crunched into an open expanse; peddling drugs, food to anyone with money able to afford them or drugs to trade. No one was anxious, it was a total love fest. People staggering about, humor abound, absurdity looking normal; practicing what we preach. Let me see your happy face?

Could this be a vision into what Gods heaven offers, be like? Everyone happy to meet one another, shaking hands, instant friendships, the desire to be loving, the hugging happening all around me. How can I help you, the message in the wind. I'll take the disaster area over the normal structures of society. We were free and we knew it! Free to speak freely! All safe spaces here, no space left, spaced out.

As for the law, they were practically nonexistent in the heart of the festival, don't recall seeing any law in the mist of it all, extinct. They were not needed; we policed ourselves. They were on the periphery taking it all in, never to forget. An example the world should take notice of. The power of self-induced Love, the happiness our souls crave, how our souls were made, with LOVE. Not the perversity we live with today. The condition, the shape I'm in. In 1973, we were not sheep, we were not victims. Son of a gun, gonna have big fun.

Tim leading the way, watermelon on his broad shoulder, the girls and I would follow Tim to an unknown designated area in this massive mound of humanity. When we find it, we will know it; was Tim's approach to the best place to settle into. Mark our spot; plant ourselves, let it grow, loving the ones we were with. Once we staked our claim, I fell asleep. Looking at the stage, we were on the left side facing it, here's looking at you Jerry Garcia. I could still see the fence to the emergency area with the helicopters saving lives; taking people to the nearest hospital, fix their broken bones, calming down excess drugs, women giving life to babies. Dear doctor, modern medicine rocking and rolling.

Patiently waiting, the audience came alive all around us, whooping and hollering a cheerful response, our morning wakeup call at 10 AM. Get the morning messages from promoter Bill Graham representing promoters Shelly Finkel & Jim Koplick. The sun shining brightly, a beautiful July morning in upstate New York. The sounds of the musicians tuning up, tweaking us; in anticipation of Uncle Johns Band. May the music never stop; in a place where there was one way out to the endless highway. The road goes on forever; as does the boundless sight of the audience, beyond the horizon where unknown dimensions orbit eternity.

I stood up, taking a 360 degree look at the sea of flesh as far as I could see in every direction under the blue sky. How could I adequately describe what I was looking at? How did we get this close into the action? In the middle of it all, the eye of the tiger. I didn't have two coins in my pockets to rub together, I was the richest man in the world, experiencing something that was priceless. Don't want your money, don't want your time, just want a good time. I took a sip from the loving cup.

On the speakers, promoter Bill Graham admonishing people for hanging out too long on the ass hole pole. A place to climb high up, look to the horizon, see the enormity of the event. Backed up by a 50,000-watt state of the art sound system. Noon time, The Grateful Dead performed their happy music, with sadness, their beloved Pig Pen aka, Ronald Charles McKernan would not be there; having passed away March 8, 1973. The look of a Bulldog, the affectionate presence of a velvety Pitbull puppy. So high above us, his watchful eyes; the music plays on.

Indeed, the music never stopped on the way to Terrapin Station, via "Summer Jam 73." The Grateful Dead played for a long time in the blistering heat, performing valiantly, they withered under the hot New York summer sun. As their time on stage was coming to an end, it looked like rain was on the horizon, after going through fire on the mountain. It's HHHHOT!

Next up, The Band. People wondering, where's Bob Dylan? At home changing diapers, a family man with children to raise. Not up on cripple creek springing a leek with the rest of us. I was most familiar with "The Band." While in high school, during library time, I would listen to albums with headphones by the Band from our music collection in the sound room. Different from all the stuff we heard on AM radio in 1970. FM radio was just beginning to take off, the future accelerating, the speed of light upon us.

Crocodile Dundee must have felt the same thing when he first entered Manhattan, New York. How many hands can I shake today? From our spot, the stage was a not far away to the eyes, amazing. In terms of the vastness of the crowd, we were right on top of the stage. Making friends for all America to see. The kids are alright, it was 1973.

The speakers towering over us from high above the grounds perpetuating the sound, the speakers further and further away from the stage, seemingly all the way to the horizon, that's how many people congregated "Summer Jam 73." Still alive and well, every now and then I know it's kinda hard to tell, but we were all still alive and well.

Phil Walden, the president of Capricorn Records and

the manager of The Allman Brothers Band quoted in Rolling Stone magazine, stated, "680,000 people attended," was the consensus number of the audience. Others say, "One million;" give or take a thousand or two. The second largest city in New York state for three days. Then there were none. The mess afterword's was epic. If you could think it, it was probably left behind. Just my imagination, running away with me. Treasure hunt.

"The Band" took to the stage, on the horizon, dark angry clouds headed our way, a cool change is coming. Back on our feet again, people frolicking to the sounds of the melodic music played with a passionate pursuit of perfection. Sky divers overhead leaping into the party, no ticket needed. The Band played on, the storm moved closer; Levon Helm fascinated, watching the jumpers from his perch behind his drums, leap out of the plane!

Levon speaking to the audience, marveling at the sight of it all, "I wish I could do that!" What Levon didn't know; one of the paratroopers after leaping out of the plane lit a flare with 4 ounces of Military explosive TNT in it. Theatrics to his detriment. His Jump suit caught fire; he landed in the woods about a half mile from the concert site. Stunning those close to the impact, the rest of us not knowing the tragedy that took place, while babies were being born amongst us. Life and death converging at "Summer Jam 73." The sky diver; Willard "Smitty" Smith of Syracuse, New York. In remembrance of "Smitty."

The Band in fine form, evident they were having as much fun as the audience. Laughing and joking around, ominously, the skies opened up on us. I could see rain drops dancing off the end of the grand piano; darkness enveloped the festival; there was no escape from it. Copious amounts of water cascading down from the clouds onto the people, the spirit in the sky bursting. Dramatic violent, lightning crashes, it was now a sky show delivered by mother nature. The unwanted guest, expressing her emergence into the party.

The Band had to vacate the stage area for sanctuary in the trailor compound behind the stage, in a massive no trespassing territory for the bands and their crews. Their home for the duration of the event, they were trapped in like the rest of us, helicopters, their only way out. It was not time to go! The musicians, pop a top on a tiny, I have another blow. For the rest of us standing by, there was nowhere to seek shelter from the storm.

Out of nowhere people were passing around giant clear plastic tarps, big enough for fifty people to stand under. We held our hands high, holding up the plastic tarps protecting us from a total monsoon drenching. Only the mud at our feet was wet, packing in closer and closer to one another. Getting to know you! When my arms got tired, I let them down, resting, so many people taking turns holding their arms up, we did not get soaked to the bone. I had no complaints, the voluptuous girl in the bathing suit behind me getting ever closer to me, pressed up against my back. I turned to look at her, her rubescent smile told me she liked it, I did too.

Once again, "The Band" took to the stage, lightening stopped, the flash storm passed us by making it safe to get back up on the stage with all the electronics; for a while there, it was deadly scary. Rick Danko the bass player sang, "Raining in my Heart," appropriate and moving rendition of a lovely Buddy Holly song. The Band resuming their pulsating melodic rhythms, we boogied on till the rest of their set was done, concluding the sound of music. Hit me with music, well it makes you feel OK!

Another break in the performances, people started moving in every direction, like homing birds walking back to their camp sites or just trying to get some breathing space from the cramped quarters we were in. Temperature starting to cool down, the mist came off the wet ground. At that point, I lost big Tim Marchase with the co-eds, started making my way back to the U-Haul rental truck , see if we had any food left, take a break, feeling scorched and soggy. It was a long grind from the time we left Edinboro via Jamestown to Watkins Glen. Youth was not wasted on us.

On my way there, a petite slender girl with shoulder length brownish red hair and the most beautiful green eyes I had ever seen, started talking to me as we walked along. "You talking too me?" And she was! She was a "Dead Head," her reason for being there. Like everyone else, she was hungry. Asking me if I could feed her. I told her about the truck and the food we brought, she decided to come along with me. On the way there, we bumped into two guys wrapped in a soaked sleeping bag, holding each other up; they were so dark from the sun, they looked like burnt toast. Both claimed to be taxicab drivers from New York city. They too, were hungry.

They made me a proposition. Pulling a sandwich baggy out of a soaked pocket, one of them says, "it's smokin Opes." "What's that," I asked? "Opium, you can smoke in a pipe," the other one says. Time to be educated. "Will trade for food!" "Give us something we can eat; we will share it with you." I never smoked opium before, never even saw it from anyone I knew or met in my early hippie days. "OK," I said, "but I can't guarantee what is left at our truck.

Come along, we will see." Together the four of us slogged our way around the emergency area with the tents and helicopters, on around to the U-Haul rental truck, next to the cyclone fence. Where my clan was gathering, shaking the wet off, like a shaggy dog. I invited them into the back of the truck, fortunately there were candy bars left, not much of anything else for us to consume or snicker to.

It was good enough for the two taxicab drivers, they chomped down on Mars candy bars, the green-eyed girl had a Milky Way. Cabbies; sitting down breaking out the pipe, an opium break. The four of us taking turns hitting on the pipe, everyone else in their own state of reality. I have to say, the opium high was pleasant and psychedeli-cized. I said to the people in the back of the truck, keep them cigarettes going. Turns out, it was only one cigarette looking like six cigarettes, the buzz was that good, and mellow. Never smoked opium since that day, a rare event for me.

The content green-eyed girl, and I decided to move our party to the under belly of the rental truck (aint that loving you baby). Later on, now in darkness, I woke up to the sound of John Rice calling my name. "Ron, Ron, wake up, The Allman Brothers Band are getting ready to come on stage, we got to go man." Waking up to an eigengrau of darkness, the girl with the green eyes was gone. I won't forget her; aint no sunshine when the sparkling in her eyes is gone. Mike Walsh standing there with his hands in his pockets smiling at me. Deciding to join them for skullduggery; we moved out.

The New York night cooled down, muddy, soggy bottom, we made our way past the emergency area; looking past the cyclone fence as the helicopters were coming and going, taking people to better care at hospitals, returning for more. This was now a city with all the demands a city makes on society. The moment seemed like it was part of a dramatic movie as the helicopters barely cleared the tops of the trees on their way out looking desperate to get out of there for the hospitals. Inspite of its city size, only one person died from a stabbing. Not bad odds for 680,000 human beings, and then some.

We walked along the fence guiding us to the back end of it, adjacent to the stage. As long as we straddled the fence, we had easy passage. John and Mike had other motives I was Shanghaied into. In the background, we could hear Sam Cutler, the Grateful Dead's manager introduce The Allman Brothers Band, as they broke into "Wasted Words." Scattered like lost words, soundtrack in the background, we headed towards our mission. Walking along the fence running the length of the stage and the compound the musicians held court in. John Rice says, "we should sneak under the fence; forget being out front with everyone else. We would crash the party backstage; see how the other half lives."

I was thinking why not, Duane Allman would not be there to play for us, it hadn't been two years (10/29/71) since Duane died in a motorcycle accident living in Macon, Georgia. A sad heart-breaking day. The hurt never goes away. The music lives on, so did we. After Wasted Words, ABB paused for the legendary promoter Bill Graham, individually introducing the Allman Brothers Band. They whipped into a great version of, "Done Somebody wrong."

What struck me as much as the size of the crowd; what my eyes witnessed in the wooded forest directly behind the stage compound. Looking into the deep darkness of the forest. As far as I could see, were campfires, they appeared to be infinite with no end to them; on and on they went into the vastness into deep darkness. Absolutely mind blowing. Like being in another world, I will never know or experience in this lifetime. Imagine what heaven and eternity must be like. Every now and then, God gives us a glimpse, helping us keep the faith.

Guided along the fence, we came to a spot someone breached. The bottom of the fence was bowed up, a body size bend in it. Like someone slid under the fence. Someone small like me, 135 pounds. John Rice says let's do it here. Mike looking on, he was game. I said, "OK, since I'm the smallest, I'll hold the fence up, you guys go first." Mike Walsh slid under, stood there while I held the cyclone fence up for John Rice, who resembled the former football Steeler, Troy Polamalu. He needed more clearance.

John halfway under when out of the dark, this hippie guy runs up to us, stopping John. Busted, we could go no further. John backed out, then Mike, I muscled the fence again. I asked the security guy what Band he was with. He said, "The Allman Brothers." I asked if there were others with them from North Carolina?" People I had met along the way before this encounter, friends of the Allman Brothers Band. He said, "everyone here is from Macon." Then asks John Rice for a cigarette. John says, "get yer own."

It's just as well, now we go out front, see what all the excitement is about; we were hearing from behind the stage. I could feel it. Continuing on towards the other end of the stage, we popped out about fifty yards from the front of the right side of the stage. There he was, majestically sitting behind his nine-foot grand piano; Chuck Leavell, rolling melodies through them Ivory keys. I stepped into an energy source that would affect the path of my life. A sense of purpose in myself from this event came over me. I had been floundering my way through a young life, aimlessly wondering. The seed was planted, now it slowly begins to grow. Time is on my side, yes, it is.

The stage seemed higher than most, because of the

massive crowd. Seemed like the Allman Brothers Band were playing in the clouds. Looking up to see them. Standing there in the cool New York summer night; mud up to our ankles, audience hypnotized, beyond description. It was a spiritual soulful event taking hold of nearly a million people all at once, our collective kinetic energy bonding us together. The new beginning when the distance from the microphone on stage to the furthest person back, changed forever, the end of an era. There was mega money to be made from here on out.

At this spot in the crowd, we settled in. A chance to focus on the energy of this music. My first time witnessing it. The Allman Brothers Band were all business. The audience transposed into hypnosis; we would follow this music anywhere it led us. The musicians heightened sense of a historical moment would never be duplicated; they were it! So high above us.

Then the sound system went to shit for a minute before someone fixed it, the band played on, focusing on their monitors to get them past the audio noise in the sound system. The audience unconcerned, we were in our glory. Collectively we were having an out of body experience. Forever bonded by this time and place, "Summer Jam 73." No other musical experience came close, a truly blessed event meant for all of us to experience. We will never pass this way again. How the heaven did we get here?

A fantastic version of "Trouble no more," followed "Come and go Blues", a sultry version of the song that kept us bobbing up and down, mud what mud, we be jamming. Dickie Betts the maestro; pulling the band along, his intensity evident, what natural charisma I thought, who is this guy? Just as I was thinking that; the guy in front of me leans to his buddy next to him. Gets close to his ear and says, "man, that Dickie Betts sure can play guitar." Then the band went into a most beautiful version of "Blue Sky." Chuck Leavell's ringing piano rolling the melodies off at the touch of his fingers, belissimo. His piano taking the parts Duane Allman played on the original recordings. A cool rendition and appropriate, no one could replace the sound of Duane Allmans guitar.

Dickie Betts: when he wasn't casually strolling the stage, stood tall before the microphone, like a matador, confident. He held command of center stage, the only guitar player up there masterfully filling all the spaces between the lyrics and the other musicians pulsating churning sound, hitting the note.

When the song ended, I asked John Rice who is Dickie Betts? He said, "the other guitar player, Chuck Leavell took Duane Allmans place in the band." The rest of the history.

The Allman Brothers broke into "One way out." John Checks to see what time it was. Too bad, a decision was made back at the truck before we left for the Allman Brothers set; for us to pull out of the disaster area by midnight; beat the rush, if there was one. Many would be paralyzed, others never wanting to leave this place, felt like heaven. All the love you've been giving, has all been meant for you.

Reluctantly, we had to go! Felt like a near death experience where we are told it's not our time to die; you must go back to time and space. There's more for you to do.

Moving through the denseness of the people, stepping over, on people, bobbing and weaving, bumping and grinding our way out of there, no one seemed to be annoyed with our aggressive jaunt through the crowd; eyes fixated on the stage. We could not be left behind. If we were, it would be an adventure getting back to Edinboro; we may not have had the energy or stamina for. Would have been interesting, that is for sure, for what it's worth. Who we would meet, how would they help us home; it's a long way there.

The entourage waiting for our return not wanting to leave us behind, relieved seeing us turn the corner at the back of the U-Haul truck, sheer joy on our faces, we made it. That loving feeling was not lost on everyone. If I could have one wish from God, ask to go back to that place in time, do it again: like Ground hog day. Everyone loaded up in the rental truck; in the midnight moonlight John Drago put it in gear. The music still emanating in the background, people yelling, clapping thunderously. We leave the way we came, on the high road through the audience, again. Was it a near death experience? Hard to exit Heaven.

I was back in the same place at the back of the truck, door cracked open, still listening as the Allman Brothers Band introduced, "Ramblin Man." How appropriate, we were rambling on out of there. We would never be the same. The further away we got from the stage, the music would go on; till the Allman Brothers Band finished playing. Afterwards, the big Jam happened. We missed it; like the epic sound check the night before. All three bands packed themselves onto the stage pulling off a massive jam. Some say the Grateful Dead where tripping, others, "The Band" were drunk and the Allman Brothers Band, well, they were all coked up.

They couldn't get their drugs together. Listening to the jam later on, it wasn't noticeable, but some say it may have been. While we were in Jamestown city jail, the night before, an epic Jam took place as a sound check, because New York state law said their permit was for July 28th. By law, not allowed to perform on the 27th. They found a way to skate the law and the rules, extended sound check, by jam.

I am no critic, just a man with a serious appetite for Rock and Roll music. In the back of the truck, we were all looking for the movie cameras; had to be a movie we were tricked into doing. No one bothered telling us the plot, we manufactured up our own plot. I kept asking Mya, "were are the cameras hidden." Mya said, "sitting on top of the world Ronnie, on top of the world." We were so free in 1973! How did we lose our way? What the hell happened to us? The technological blues. Sing us home.

The next thing we know, the U-Haul truck pulls off interstate 79 onto Pa. 6N east into Edinboro, it was a sunny 11:30 AM July 29th, 1973, don't let the sun go down on us. We want to keep this precious memory in our souls, do it all over again in our dreams, though we would go our separate ways; this event would bond our lives together forever.

CHAPTER EIGHT

With our great escape from "Summer Jam 73," we had the rest of the summer, create more positive joy at "Char Lynn." August, how are we going to top what happened on our way to "Summer Jam 73?" We didn't! Our climax to the summer of 1973 had come and gone. Aint no bread left in the bread box. There would be no sequel to "Summer Jam 73." Nor would there be another summer or year quite like 1973. Soon disco music would pervade into the commercial music scene, changing the landscape and direction. Songs like "Rubber Band Man," "Please don't go!" "Don't leave me this way," "Kiss and say goodbye." Four gems the disco era left us with. A time and place for everything. There is a season for everything. That's all right by me.

Taking each day one at a time, I had to consider where do I go from here, my whole life in front of me. Having no plans for the future, youth, got in my way of thinking. Always up against myself. Once August was over and the congregating at "Char Lynn" eased up, a new school year beginning. I would have to find another home and a job, a sense of direction. Soon my mentor and best buddy Joey David would embark on his mission to Pergamino, Argentina.

He would be gone till spring of 1974. He was up against it, the 27-man law firm from in Pergamino where out to trick him. Steal his inheritance with handshakes and smiles on their faces while they attempt to do it. They would use the back taxes owed to heist his property. Like James Bond, Joey entering the scene, vowed this would not happen, situated in his boldest element; play the game, outthink them!

The rest of the summer much the same as June and July. The future, what to do with it, made callings on all of us. We can't live vicariously indefinitely, or can we? Observations and opinions about being responsible would creep into conversations by people on the outside of the family wanting to participate; then cautioning us about what to do next with our lives. They meant well providing good example of themselves. Still, we were young, those things would have to wait for some of us. Others grew up, pointing themselves in a legitimate direction. Looking for meaning in our lives in a world governed by evil. A world where we bend and shape things any way, we want them to be. No accountability.

One of my lasting fond memories of the summer of 1973 was how much latitude the local police and authorities allowed us to get away with. Really, astonishing how much freedom they looked away from; we peacefully ruled the town of Edinboro. The Friday of the Labor day weekend, students returned to Edinboro for fall classes. All of us, it was a big lot, spending the summer together; gathered in the town center across the street from The Edinboro Hotel Bar. A place were five roads intersect, the apex and climax of our summer, 1973.

We were drinking cans of beer out in the open on the corner; the crowd puffed up, getting larger and larger, spreading up and down Meadville street. Enough cash put up for 12 cases of beer neatly stacked on the sidewalk: cooler with ice next to it, our Mardi Gras in Edinboro. Of course, very illegal. The Edinboro police in the cruiser would slowly pass us by; give us a curious look, smile, wave to everybody as we respectfully lifted our beers to the officer. It was laid back, it was 1973. One of the great years in American history.

The scuttlebutt on the street; Jimmy Bruce (J.B.) was busted for a quantity of pot. A sign that the party was coming to a close. Couldn't put that cork back in the bottle. Labor day weekend would mark the end of it. With no prospects of how to proceed, no vehicle to help me do it; accepting a friends offer, ride to Florida. Make a go of it there, winter's coming. I had nothing to lose, an adventure to gain. I knew people in Lake Wales, revisit that place one more time. Besides, Buffy Williams would be there at her father and stepmothers house for the winter in Babson Park. Red neck capital of the south. That's what love will make you do, a hullaballoo.

Students living off campus, those living in the houses lined up along Ontario street would arrive early for fall semester in an attempt to fix this old house up. Lots of cleaning, painting, holes to patch and arrangements made to make their stay comfortable as they could; like being comfortably numb at home. The house to the left of "Char Lynn" was being prepared by 6 girls, neighbors residing there. The place needed intense renovations. Requiring what would be 3 days and nights, cleaning the carpets, painting the walls, getting the stench out from the previous tenants: the smell of beer, furniture arrangements etc. They were busy Bees those girls next door.

They used mothers little helper to get it all done on time for their open house party Saturday night, Labor Day weekend. I would be there along with others from "Char Lynn," neighborly, to help them celebrate the coming school year. The way the house was physically arranged, when entering the narrow doorway leading to a passageway upstairs to the bedrooms and bathroom. To the left was the big living room and to the back of the building was the kitchen and dining room, with bathroom. There was another room to the right as one entered the house. It was a small room, off to the side, a miniature living room or sitting room for reading. I took up a spot in there planting myself in a chair next to the opening to the hallway leading upstairs.

Music blasting, people congregating, the house was a rockin, the people were a boppin. Beer and wine flowing, everyone having a great time with their choice of drugs and perspective partners, music setting the tone. I settled into a chair after ingesting one of my "THC" tabs. "Chock full of Nuts coffee" wasn't the only thing delivering that heavenly feeling. With all the fun and games going on around me, I was content to drift into a blissful corner in my mind. A perch I scoped the girls out from, melting into my chair. Here I am!

Out of the bliss, came a screeching sound, a young women in despair, running from the living room to the stairwell to the bedrooms upstairs. Happening fast, looking to see what the commotion was all about, disturbing the peace. Watching the girl, her name, Mary Krevaneak from Pittsburgh; turn the corner jutting herself upon the steps in a frantic pace to get away from someone. At the same time, see this big arm reaching for her legs, clipping her feet by the ankles. Making Mary trip, lose her balance, fall, banging the side of her head onto the handrail attached to the wall.

Apparently, a big guy, formerly a football player for the Edinboro Fighting Scots was the culprit making Mary trip. She was not interested in his advances towards her. He couldn't take the rejection, becoming more aggressive with Mary; till she had no choice but to run from him. Right past me. I did not see Mary strike her head on the railing, though another girl, one of her roommates did, from the landing upstairs. When Mary reached the top of the staircase, blanking out, she did a complete circle spin, dropped to her butt, Mary began to shake uncontrollably, convulse, her faced turning blue, gasping for air.

In the moment, I didn't think it was much more than any other rejection I had seen at parties including my own rejections; till I heard the scream of another girl at the top of the steps. Then I knew something terrible was happening, I could no longer sit idlily by. I lunged forward out of my seat; looked to the top of the stairs, seeing Mary's eyes rolling back in her head; convulsing, shaking uncontrollably, turning blue from a lack of oxygen. Instinctively, I knew what had to be done. My "High" was on hold, my mind interrupted the soulful feeling I had, get off that cloud, go save Mary, her life is in danger.

No one knew what was happening, or what to do about it, the intense seriousness of it all. Life and death, an uninvited guest, the grim reaper entered the party. Running to the top of the staircase, I got on my knees, reached for Mary's mouth, hard as I was trying to open Mary's mouth, I could not get past her clenched teeth, grinding away. Time was running out; brain damage will ensue. Racing against the clock, my fingers being chewed up, the guy next to me holding Mary's hand telling Mary everything would be alright. I kept trying to get my fingers into Mary's mouth. Fearful if I could not open her mouth, I would have to break her teeth to get at her tongue. I learned this in high school health class.

It was life or death, no time for 911, I had to act. Everyone that could fit into the bottom of the stairwell anxiously watching me work my fingers into Mary's mouth. All the girls were crying, others in shock, mood changer. A tragedy about to take place. I could not let that happen. I was built to thrive in times of adversity. Right were God wanted me to be. I went to work.

Stubbornly, I forced two of my bloody fingers into

Mary's mouth, pressed down on her tongue dislodging it, her tongue flopped back into the front of her mouth; air now flowing into her lungs again. The guy holding Mary's hand was right after all. Everything was going to be alright. Color not blue was now flushing through Mary's cheeks, her eyes back in place, dazed, disorientated, in a state of confusion. I stayed with her, stroked her head, hugged her, gave her all my love, praying she would not relapse.

No one knew what to think about what just happened, so sudden. The blow to her head with three days of stimulants, an effort to stay awake; combined with lack of sleep, set Mary up for the fall. A car was summoned, take Mary to the Edinboro campus infirmary; her roommates insisting I go along just in case she had a relapse on the way there. When Mary's helpless roommates walked her to the infirmary door, I remained back at the car watching; coming to terms with what happened. Mary confused, broke loose from her handlers, pausing, turning to take a look back at me; our eyes met. I melted, when it hit me, my knees became weak; I had a mild shake to my body, the "THC" tab I took no longer had any effect on me, perhaps helping me stay calm. That night: I was where I was supposed to be.

Leaving Mary behind for observation at the infirmary for the night, we returned to the party. I left the party for home, repair my hand; I had no more words to say, grateful to God it ended well for Mary Krevaneak. A little brown-haired girl with a sweet personality, she lives. The reality of it all made me want to go somewhere, be alone with God. Why me Lord?

The week after Labor day weekend, my friend from Erie, Dave Gromacki, a Polish boy with the stereo typical nose, blond hair, an unattractive guy who was lost in life; looked to me for guidance. Pointed ourselves southbound in his 1969 Mustang fastback, his pride and joy; it was time for us to fly. Dave quit his career, or I should say job for life at Hammermill Paper Company in Erie.

His father was a lifer there. It was crazy taking off for Florida not knowing if we had enough money for gas to get there; food and drink an afterthought. Young, dumb and numb. I've always had a sense that I would be protected, I had no fear, can't speak for what Dave was thinking. What was he running from? Not long after we crossed the Florida state line from Georgia, we picked up a hitchhiker going to Orlando; same place we were headed, right back to the boarding house. The oasis I stayed at the prior winter, sort things out from there. End of the line?

Our rider was a military guy on his way home, on leave from the Navy, sail on Sailor. Good thing we picked him up. We were low on cash and gas. When the Sailor knew our predicament, he offered up enough money for gasoline insuring we would make it to Orlando without being completely broke. We dropped him off at another highway he needed to continue for the last leg to his destination.

We limped on into Orlando with our tails between our legs. Turns out the boarding house was now a place of the Lord. A sanctuary for the lost souls wandering into Florida from parts unknown. They called it, "The Shiloh House." We were welcomed in, they fed us, calmed our fears. Though they said our stay could not be for long unless we did some tasks around the Shiloh House or labored in the Orange fields. We could stay longer just as long as we turned our wages over to them, trapped. Might have been OK in the short term, the long term, not so much.

It was a place to meet other people searching for a way through life after venturing into Florida. A transient place:

with its own dangers, if one did not think clearly, watching their back. In that world, people are always on the take and nobody you meet is really your buddy. Everyone has an angle. Let your guard down, you will find yourself running down the street, looking for the friend that just ripped you off, cussing up a storm. Survival instincts reducing humanity to its lowest level of form.

After being at the Shiloh house for three days, lounging, feeding, our time had run out. After coming up with enough cash, we devised a plan, drive to the east coast, around Cocoa, Florida, see what we could make of it there. It was a chance, though no different than the one we took going to Orlando; a place to be leary of in the early 1970's. Orlando was a growing metropolis attracting a lot of unsavory characters. One could say Dave and I were just two more of them. We were two honest guys, that would disqualify Dave and me from unsavory.

With just enough money for gas, a few days of food and beer, we took a leap into the unknown believing everything would be alright, someone would help us, my faith in God at play. In our desperation, we met a character like I mentioned, a trickster. Fooled us for the cost of a few cocktails at a beach bar; said he had a place for us to stay taking advantage of our desperate generosity. It was bogus, Dave wanted to kick his ass, I said let it go, we won't get fooled again.

We left that bar, wandering next door to a beachfront hotel, took a seat on the sand close to the breakers coming in with the high tide; wondering where do we go from here? Stumped, we had no ideas or schemes to make it through this night. I became thirsty, deciding to take a chance with a total stranger. Knock on a beach front hotel room door; ask for a glass of water, no real sense of awareness about how I looked in that situation. It was 1973, grasping for a miracle, I'd witnessed them before, still believing.

Knock on the door, a 21-year-old good-looking friendly girl opens it. She's all alone, thank God we were honorable people, she was safe opening the door for us. I asked for a glass of water telling her I was very thirsty, why, I, a stranger would knock on her door. She relaxed sensing I was a good guy. We began to make conversation like we had always known each other. Dave stood on the landing outside her door, witnessing this transcendent moment.

In the short time I talked with her, making conversation, she said she was from Orlando. I asked if she knew the guy, I was looking for from Meadville the winter before, with the boys from Meadville, Pa. I told her his name. I found my miracle; though it wasn't the one I was looking for. Turns out, she knew the guy, though not all that well. I was making conversation to get past my loneliness. She had a comforting effect, the touch of a women. She said, last year at the time me and the Meadville boys were looking for him, a place we could get started in Florida; he was in the hospital.

Mangled, nearly killed in an automobile accident. Was in the hospital for many months; she went on to say. Same time we showed up in Orlando, why we could not locate him. It was interesting to find out the answer to that mystery, though I was not searching for it. This would be a reoccurrence in my life, meeting people in faraway places I knew or someone they knew that I knew. Into the Mystic. My natural place to be.

Running out of conversation, thanking her for the water, Dave and I left for his car. We would find a safe place for the night, sleep in the 1969 fastback Mustang. The next morning, return to the Shiloh house in Orlando, start all over from there. It was much like leaving a country, then getting a new Visa to return for three more days of comfort and sanctuary. Come up with another scheme that would propel us forward.

They let us stay, the good Christians that they tried to be. After two days, I got the idea to go to Lake Wales, an hour's drive south on Florida Highway 27 were it meets Florida highway 60. I knew people there; believing they would be an asset to us; we had a chance, going to Lake Wales. I met another homeless guy from Syracuse, New York, his name, Bob. Same predicament as Dave and me. Decided to avoid winter in New York state, traveled to Florida for work, expected the best accepting the worst, then he met me.

I told him of my adventure from the winter before, certain if we traveled to Lake Wales, we would get off this Merry Go Round; be situated. Leaving Dave behind, he was out walking the street with other homeless people, searching for an opportunity. I informed the Shiloh people what I would be doing, please let Dave Gromacki know where I went. I will return. Wrote down the Shiloh house phone number, out the door we went, hitchhiking to Lake Wales.

Got a quick ride. Once we made it to our destination, our host, who picked us up, knew Donna Storey, driving Bob and me into Lake Wales to where Donna lived; blessed again. The big affectionate girl Jim Hess introduced me to the previous winter. It was Donna's house we partied at, the place I talked Jim out of blowing his brains out, twice. Dropped off at Donna's house, though not the same place she lived the spring of 1973. Knocked on her door. She was stunned to see me again, something she never expected would happen. No Jim Hess with me. There I was, back in Lake Wales, for another winter go round, Syracuse Bob, the original Syracuse Bob, looking on. I get knocked down, I get back up again, nothing's going to keep me down.

Donna moved into an elderly women's home, renting a room. Pretty much sharing the house with the old lady. Our prospects of holding up there was out of the question. However, Donna told me my friend Stoney and his roommate Mike Ruschak, could help us. We walked over to Stoney's apartment, off highway 60. When Bob and I entered the apartment, we arrived just on time to join the party.

We were welcomed into the party, the beer and the joints floating around the living room. Once we were comfortable, I explained to Mike & Stoney what we were doing in Lake Wales. Unfortunately, there was no room at this apartment; another local guy named Jimmy Knute was sleeping on the couch. Mike suggested we walk further on up the road to Bo Bo Duffield's house; he had plenty of room for two more people in his big house. He was living in his mother's home off Highway 60 east with a fat young 16-year-old guy named Moon.

His mother moved to California; start a new life, sounds familiar. We would walk to his house; he was home along with Moon. Bo Bo was glad to see me again. I introduced him to Bob. I said, "Mike Ruschak sent us, we need a place to live and an opportunity to make an income, staying right here in Lake Wales, can you help us?" He didn't flinch, said we were welcome there as long as we needed, he wanted the company. Bo Bo was a benevolent unemployed young man, not put off by our circumstances; he understood, was happy to help. Then Moon chimed in, said he knew where Bob and I could be hired, in fact on the spot. I asked him, "where?" He said, "Heinkel and McCoy construction company.

Located at the intersection of Highway 27 and Highway 60 at the west end of town. "They always need laborer's; will hire us the same day, send us to a job site." I'd worked construction before, it was hard labor, yet a chance to get out of the hole I put myself into. Syracuse Bob was into it. We will get up early tomorrow, go do it.

All I had with me was the cloths on my body. Same for Bob. I will have to contact Dave Gromacki, let him know what we have accomplished, he will come join us; bring me my suitcase stored away in the back of his Mustang. That was the thinking. In the morning Bob and I hitchhiked to Heinkel and McCoy, a short drive to the west end of town. Just like Moon said, we were hired on the spot.

After we filled out the employment documents, social security number and all, we were given hard hats and a shovel; I'll take this job and shove it. Along with other laborer's, we loaded up into an extended white Econo Van; drove to a work site on the outskirts of south Winter Haven, Florida. We would be digging ditches for a new water line. Huge cement pipes would be fitted together in the deep ditch we were digging in. Dangerous task in Florida working in sand; cave-ins a big concern. Show me the money!

Oppressively hot, September in central Florida. There is no letup in the heat of the sun in the Florida climate. I have the ability to mentally block out the agony of the struggle. Give me a purpose, an opportunity, I will give all I got to succeed blocking out the hardships. Purposeful survival instincts will do that for you. If not, losing is what's left, I do not like losing.

Diligently working away, the ditch getting deeper, longer, the talk in the hole ever present; like we were in a chain gang. Visions of Cool Hand Luke in my mind. I could not see over the edge of the ditch. Syracuse Bob was six foot tall, not a problem for him. Wiping the sweat off our brows, moisture dripping down our backs, we would have no clean clothing to change into after the day's work was done; imperative Dave Gromacki travel to Lake Wales, I need my cloths.

Bob would have to fend for himself. Not knowing the people, he traveled with to Florida, he would be at their mercy or take the fight to the struggle. The work was hard, drenched in our own salty moisture, Bob had to have his head swirling, wondering what the hell he was doing in central Florida ditch digging, busting his butt, scorching sun beating down on him.

I was resigned to what had to be done, I would persevere. Around 11:30 AM, almost lunch time, though we had none to eat, Syracuse Bob stops digging. In a fit of frustration, anxiety launched Bob out of the ditch. Let go of his shovel, Bob slammed his hard hat on the ground. Asked, "which way is Orlando?" Someone pointed up the road next to us, "that way" he said. Syracuse Bob started walking in that direction till we could no longer see him; he disappeared from view. No one knew what to say. Then it was lunch time. Never saw Syracuse Bob again.

When I returned to Bo Bo's home after work, I called the Shiloh house in Orlando a second time; ask them if they gave my message to Dave Gromacki, I had to have my cloths. They said they had but did not know his where abouts at this time. Left me not knowing what to think about Dave. Is he coming here or not? After drying off my cloths, I would shower, then put the sweaty cloths back on.

I had a safe place to stay, a pillow to rest my head on, a job, I was not hungry. Still believing I would see Dave again. The next morning, walk the fifty yards from Bo Bo's house out onto Highway 60, put my thumb out, wait for a kind and helpful driver take pity on me, give me a ride to work; a short drive away. It happened like that. A man pulled over, I got in, he obviously was going to work himself; lunch pail sitting next to him on the front seat. I told him where I was going; he said, if I stand in the same place Monday through Friday, the same time I did today, he will take me to work without failure.

He never let me down. It was up to me to be on time. All my life I have had the good fortune of people like this kind selfless stranger come to my aid as if I made a reservation with them, a divine reservation. That's what faith will do for you. Got to stay positive. You will be served.

Dave Gromacki never made the trip to Lake Wales. I had no idea why or what happened to him, never did I see him again, not in Florida nor back in Edinboro/Erie, Pennsylvania. Off my radar, still, I had no cloths to change into. Every day, till I received my first paycheck two weeks later, I showered after work put on the sweaty cloths again. Patience, it's all temporary, preserver. It will get better in a little while.

All my clothes in my suitcase were dirty needing a laundry cleaning. The last of my clean cloths I had to wear is what I had on when I arrived in Lake Wales, not my best. I continued to loyally work with Heinkel and McCoy. Daydreaming about the possibility of seeing Buffy Williams again. This job was all I had, with no automobile for transportation, I accepted my fate.

Bide my time till I could acquire transportation, enabling me to seek other employment. For now, I would continue as I had been gutting it out, serving my purpose. Be my own hero. I'm a man, yes, I can, and I love it so. It takes patience and belief in oneself to overcome the struggles and difficulties in life that come everyone's way; there's a balance to it. There really isn't an easy street, or a life of free things, someone pays for it. In some way, in time, the perception of free comes back; the universe will be paid for its benevolent generosity, tenfold.

Getting reacquainted with the people I met the winter before in Lake Wales and nearby Babson Park, I was not alone. Mike Ruschak and Stoney where becoming my dependable buddies. September turned into October, the pay checks kept coming in, I had enough money to buy a used car.

In a "Buy Here Pay Here" lot. I came across a 1966 Bonneville. Big like an aircraft carrier with a 26-gallon gas tank. Problem was that the Arab oil embargo had begun. Though gas was 33 cents a gallon, there was no gasoline to buy. When I could, it was a dollar at a time. Get in line, back of the que.

No one got into first rights fist fights to the pump gas like they do today. It was a kinder gentler nation in 1973. Now, it's put em up. What will electric power bring us? Lights out! Was that a punch or the electric company. No, it's the government and they are here to help! For some people it doesn't matter, they are always in the dark. Free tings for them is better than being free. Not in 1973.

Now that I had an address to receive mail, I called Joey David right before he left for Pergamino Argentina, giving my Lake Wales address to him. Here's what happened during his time in South America. Joey periodically would send me a letter with newspaper clippings from Buenos Aries. The economy was failing due to enormous inflation that would become out of control of the government, wheelbarrows of money for a loaf of bread. Their world was on fire. History repeats itself, even today.

There were many terrorist bombings around Buenos Aries; the unrest was alarming; people were not happy. A government failing. Argentine currency turning to nothing or close to it. Joey had his own problems to deal with. Argentina had the failing Banks to deal with. For what it's worth.

Joey's inheritance was a block of land in the center of the business district of Pergamino, a union hall building, a large one, and a mansion his deceased grandfather lived in, was now housing the mistress of the Mayor of Pergamino. The Mayor didn't like that his girlfriend had to move out when Joey arrived in Pergamino. There were other valuable properties, though all had back tax issues. Pergamino was a city of 100,000 people in 1973, Joey's property was worth a lot ($).

All the while, he was making influential friends because of it. Even got a girlfriend named Maria, they became engaged. Her father was high up in Argentina's Aerolineas airline. They were to be married, though in the end, it did not happen. I met her in 1975, she visited Joey in Pittsburgh, together they came to see me in Edinboro.

Sadly, her life was restricted, Maria was a hemophiliac, one of five people in the world having her precise condition; I was told. For Maria to make this trip to America was a huge gamble, she loved Joey that much. Maria could not have even the slightest cut; or her life could be in danger. She loved me like a puppy. To know me is to love me.

Another friend Joey made, a wealthy inheritor himself named Willie. Willies family owned the largest trucking company in Argentina. Successful though losing money, falling through the cracks. Flustered with his inability to find the leakage in the bookkeeping. Willie asked Joey to help him. Joey did just that, going over the books he found all the discrepancies. The company was losing money

166

because of lousy managers, wasteful spending and outright theft. Joey saved the day making Willie a friend for life. Joey's high IQ, common sense, making an impression. He must be rich.

Willie introduced Joey to another wealthy family from Bariloche' in the southern part of Argentina known for all the Germans that migrated there before world war two; after the end of world war two, loyal Nazis. Very wealthy people living in a mansion. That is all I remember about their wealth, it was enormous. Joey owning the valuable property in Pergamino, made it seem as though Joey was a wealthy American.

Though all he had was his Social Security disability check, the result of incurable kidney disease. Why he had to give up being a Merchant Marine. The Germans knew nothing of it, Joey did not speak of it. If they wanted to think he was rich, he went along with it, letting them do all the talking.

Joey was the guest of honor as friends and family members gathered at the home of these wealthy Germans. Everyone sitting around a long dinner table, talking about money and politics, Joey's property, all things affluent. During the exchanges, one of the daughters asks Joey how many millions he has. Joey had to think fast, he was not prone to lying. In his mind, if they believed he was as wealthy as they were, he would let the charade continue; now he had to answer the question. It was an inappropriate question when the matriarchal mother chimed in. Millions, millions, who counts them?"

With that said, Joey laughed, they all laughed, that was the end of that. He was saved from an embarrassment. Joey asked to be excused from the table to go to the bathroom. He needed an escape just in case the daughter became aggressive, pressing her question. Joey got directions to the hallway leading to the nearest bathroom in this cavernous Mansion.

Still nervous about the question of wealth, losing his composure, forgetting what side of the hallway the bathroom door was on. Turned to his right instead of his left opening the door across from the bathroom door, on the right side of the hall. Took one step into the room (oops), to his surprise, the room was loaded with Nazi emblems, flags, pictures, Nazi paraphernalia and a shrine to Adolph Hitler.

Realizing what he had done, quickly removed himself from the doorway; just as the mother of the house rushes towards him down the hallway. She had to see him exiting the room. Joey didn't know what to say or how to conduct himself. All the matriarchal mother did was giggle at him. No worries. Avoiding another embarrassment. There's much more that happened in Argentina with Joey, though I cannot adequately remember it all arcuately. Strange days indeed!

As the days went by into weeks, October was over then November coming to an end, Mike Ruschak (a machinist) from Gary, Indiana said he would be moving. The lease was up at the apartment, he and Stoney were living in; off Highway 60. Stoney found someone to move in with at Lake Pierce, Mike, Jimmy Knute and I decided to rent a trailer out past Bok Tower, also situated close to Lake Pierce, same trailer park. December first, I left Bo Bo's house, Mike and I moved into a trailer, Jimmy Knute would stay with us temporarily on the couch. Stoney would be living a two-minute walk away, in a trailor.

From the time I arrived (mid-September) broke in Lake Wales till Christmas time, filled a refrigerator with food, saved up two hundred dollars (1973), bought a car, got a new wardrobe, met Debbie Binkley, a quasi-girlfriend. Less than four months I was able to accomplish all these things. Reason to be proud, resilient, proving faith in myself, recognizing the hand of God on my life. I was going to be alright. I had my stash; every weekend would be a good time, sometimes we did not wait for the weekend, living carefree; happy is as happy does.

So happy; I started living like I had always lived in central Florida. I have a car now, roam where I want to, all around the world. I settled for Lakeland, Florida. Trek over there to a place called the warehouse bar. Once was a Coca Cola warehouse, big place, now a night club; women, 1973 version.

Lakeland was a happening place in 1973. Going there was never with trepidation, I was comfortable being in Lakeland in 1973. One night while standing at the bar waiting for my drink, sky high on THC pill, I meet Karen Smith and her sister with friends.

Like an irrefutable over coming of my soul, Karen and I turned to each other, I clutched her, she me, in a kiss fest, the spontaneous explosion of passion overcame both of us. Pure love, no sweet talkin Romeo. What an Angel I found that night. The softness of her soul overcame me in my state of mind, Karen in her state of mind, kindred spirits finding each other.

Karen's sister entangled with an attraction for a guy who was with his associate or friend, both professionally dressed, we all left together for a local downtown motel. Ironic, we did no drugs while with them though, when they opened the trunk to their Cadillac, it was filled with duffle bags of drugs. We decided to decline their offer, so did they; we were at our destination. They were connected in a big way with drug trafficking. I brushed it off, it was time for the dawning of the day.

Karen and I saw each other again, kept in touch through the US mail over time. I visited her in Sarasota, Florida on my way back to Edinboro in spring of 1974. Ironically Karen ended up living in Pennsylvania married to a Pa. boy in central Pennsylvania. Her marriage failed; I was in limbo. She held onto me as long as she could, till she needed to return to Florida, help her sister cope with life. Moving different directions, lovers come and go, the river flows.

Karen Smith remains a fond memory of a women who wore love on her sleeve and in her eyes. Never abandoning her sister; she returned to Florida, help her sister recover her mind from emotional acuity gone from her grip. We will meet again in the place where the light shines brightly for kindred spirits.

Not long after I met Karen in Lakeland at the Coca Cola warehouse, I planned to go back to the Coca Cola warehouse bar on a Saturday night. I came down with something, not feeling too good, I changed my mind, did not go there that night. The fate of destiny in my favor, I missed a tragic event. A jealous man entered the music hall, open fired on people around his target (girlfriend), 3 people died, others wounded; I missed it, by the grace of God's watchful Angels. I do not walk alone. No longer a rock.

I left Heinkel and McCoy; St. Joe Paper company would be my new employer. I had experience from my summer (1972) working with Hammermill Paper Company in Erie, Pa. Why I was hired. Just on time for the New Year (1974) beginning. 1973 would be coming to an end. Looking back in retrospect, for me, letting go would be hard. In my soul I knew I would never know another time like 1973 again, an experience like "Summer Jam 73." Reeling in the years, time is passing; it's a good feeling to know.

New Year's Eve, Mike Ruschak would be spending the night with his cowgirl girlfriend from Lakeland, Florida. I would be spending New year's Eve alone. It was fine by me. I knew I would be listening to a live broadcast performance on the radio from the Cow Palace in San Francisco. The Allman Brothers Band closing out the year of 1973 the same way they closed out "Summer Jam 73" at Watkins Glen, New York.

How appropriate; The Allman Brothers Band in 1973 were considered the biggest draw in Rock music, no exception. It was their time to shine, God bless Duane Allmans soul, the impetus, he made it so; Dickie Betts picked up the baton, ran with it. Into our hearts and cherished memories. Music to sooth our souls.

After all ABB went through losing Duane Allman, then Berry Oakley in motorcycle accidents in Macon, Georgia, almost a year and a month apart, a half mile in distance from each other's accident. An Angels reach away. Chuck Leavell on Grand Piano, easing the pain. A special chosen person carrying divine prominence. A prince of a man who continued his exceptional musicianship with the Rolling Stones onto the Rock and Roll Hall of Fame. A pillar of character.

I bought a bottle of Vodka, complimented by orange juice, turned the radio on, kicked back into my bed, fired up a joint, listening in to one of the best performances the Allman Brothers Band ever performed for all the radio listeners to treasure. There were many guest artists performing that night. Story be told, the Grateful Dead were there as well though they would not be performing. Instead, they would be pranksters, roving suitors. Cousins to The

Allman Brothers Band, sharing the same audiences.

The second half of the 4-hour performance, Jerry Garcia and Bill Kreutzmann were on stage. Boz Scaggs sang too, wailing away in a drunken attempt to woo the crowd. Before the show, everyone in the Allman Brothers Band and their crew were put on notice by Twiggs Lyndon, ABB Road first Road Manager and sound technician, (Duane Allmans right hand man). Don't drink anything from the cooler nor stick your hands into the ice water, pull out a beer.

The Pranksters dosed everything with LSD. Butch Trucks one of the ABB drummers figured he would beat them by having his own personal bottle of Mateus wine right next to his drum kit; he would drink from it, play it safe. No LSD on me mate!

What Butch didn't know, Ken Kesey's squirt gun was invading the top of his bottle with LSD dosed water, contaminating his wine. As the show went on, the acid took effect, Butch watched his drums melt before his eyes. Not able to continue, fortunately along for the fun, Bill Stewart, a drummer and a friend of the Allman Brothers Band; sat in for Butch.

Not sure how many members of the Allman Brothers Band did not finish the show because of the mind-bending drug. I was altering my mind back at Lake Pierce, Florida. Laying right here in heaven. Bottle of Vodka by my side, orange juice for enhancement; the radio rocking my soul. My last thoughts: "what a fitting way to end the year of 1973; no regrets. Standing on the Moon, I would let the world go by; never gonna pass this way again." Love can endure, you know it will. Stay tuned; there is more.

Four hours twenty-three minutes and 30 seconds after

the show started; in the wee hours of January 1, 1974, the big jam with all the musical guests was over. With a mellow smile on my face, content, the last thing I remember hearing before I faded away into 1974. Dickie Betts thanking the audience for coming. Said, "Thank you very much folks, happy new year; Jerry Garcia, Bill Kreutzmann, Jai Johnny Johnson, Chuck Leavell, Dickey Betts, thank you; we've had a great time; good night."

WE WHERE SO FREE, IN 1973. Selah.

The story in this book is dedicated to the memory of Karen Hufnagel of Irwin Pennsylvania. Murdered April 13, 1977, in Edinboro, Pennsylvania. To this day a cold case murder in Erie County Pennsylvania. Gone, will not be forgotten. God Bless her lovely soul.

Trailer that replaced Karen Hufnagel's burnt down trailer. Identical to the one she was murdered in April 1977. The lot was vacant in 2022.

CPSIA information can be obtained
at www.ICGtesting.com
Printed in the USA
JSHW060454130723
44662JS00005B/216

9 781954 617698